Junior NKIERE MAKOLONI

COMPUTER COURSES FIRST YEAR CG

Junior NKIERE MAKOLONI

COMPUTER COURSES FIRST YEAR CG

ScienciaScripts

Imprint
Any brand names and product names mentioned in this book are subject to trademark, brand or patent protection and are trademarks or registered trademarks of their respective holders. The use of brand names, product names, common names, trade names, product descriptions etc. even without a particular marking in this work is in no way to be construed to mean that such names may be regarded as unrestricted in respect of trademark and brand protection legislation and could thus be used by anyone.

Cover image: www.ingimage.com

This book is a translation from the original published under ISBN 978-620-6-72009-6.

Publisher:
Sciencia Scripts
is a trademark of
Dodo Books Indian Ocean Ltd. and OmniScriptum S.R.L publishing group

120 High Road, East Finchley, London, N2 9ED, United Kingdom
Str. Armeneasca 28/1, office 1, Chisinau MD-2012, Republic of Moldova, Europe
Managing Directors: Ieva Konstantinova, Victoria Ursu
info@omniscriptum.com

Printed at: see last page
ISBN: 978-620-8-51200-2

Contents

PREFACE

Since the discovery of computers, many everyday activities have been simplified. Today, people can easily process information using software and computer networks. Given its evolution, this system characterises the majority of large companies, whatever their sector of activity.

It is therefore vital for students to have a certain level of computer literacy if they are to succeed in the workplace.

Possible future uses of IT

The last ten years alone have seen a major evolution in computing, with the creation of new devices to replace or complement those already in existence. These new devices are characterised by their practicality and more efficient data storage and processing capacity.processing capacity.

By analysing these changes, specialists can anticipate the possible future uses of IT, and many of them support the idea that in the near future data curation will become a more global trend, and that information gathering will become even more important.

SUMMARY

Everyone knows that information technology can improve productivity and organisation. It enables employees to use effective time-saving tools to carry out their daily tasks: word-processing tools, management software, information retrieval, task automation, and so on. For this reason, this manual, designed for students in the first year of humanities, enables all students to master the general concepts of computing and to create files and folders, to create files and folders in a computer, to draw up order forms and invoices using a computer, to master the basics of word processing and to use the Internet to make contact with third parties.

Nowadays, most employees have at least one computer at their workstation. To save money, and although some companies use Linux or IOS, most of these computers use a Windows-type operating system. The latter is particularly **vulnerable to viruses and other cyber attacks**. This can slow down employees' work and endanger the company's entire IT network. Aging or obsolete office equipment and inefficient IT tools can also lengthen tasks and limit the company's productivity.

OBJECTIVES

GENERAL OBJECTIVE

By the end of the first year of the business and management humanities, the learner will be able to use IT tools for basic tasks.

SPECIFIC OBJECTIVES

At the end of this course, any student who has followed this course assiduously will be able to :

- Master the general concepts of computing and create files and folders;
- Creating files and folders on a computer ;
- Drawing up purchase orders and invoices using the computer;
- Master the basics of word processing ;
- Using the Internet to make contact with third parties

CHAPTER I

IT CONCEPTS

1.1. DEFINITION

The term "computer science" was first used in 1962 by Philippe Dreyfus to describe the automatic processing of information.

This new word comes from the combination of two words, "information" and "automatic".

In 1967, the Academie franpaise defined computer science as "the science of the rational processing, in particular with the aid of automatic machines, of information, considered as the basis of knowledge in the scientific, economic and social fields".

Computer science can also be defined as the science of automatic and rational processing of information, considered as the basis of knowledge and communication.

1.2. ROLE

IT plays many roles in the world of modern business. Almost all businesses and companies currently use IT equipment to meet their internal and external production and case processing needs. IT is therefore the basis of a company's information circulation or processing system, hence the importance of IT in business. IT enables the databases and electronic information of a business, a company or a group to be updated. IT is therefore the medium that enables modern businesses to evolve and develop freely.

1.3. HISTORY

For thousands of years, man has created and used tools to help him calculate. Initially, most societies probably used the hand, as well as other parts of the body, as calculation aids. (It's interesting to note that the word "calculation" comes from the Latin word *calculi*, meaning "stones".) The first example of a more complex tool was the abacus, which took various forms, right up to the abacus still used in China and Russia. Among the oldest algorithms are tables dating from the time of Hammurabi (c. 1750).

Around 1617, John Napier invented a kind of perfected abacus. In 1625, his invention of logarithms enabled William Oughtred to develop the slide rule, which was used by many engineers right up until the advent of pocket calculators. For example, many of the calculations required for the Apollo programme were carried out using slide rules.

The first programmable machines

In 1725, Basile Bouchon, a Lyonnais, developed a system for

programming a loom using a perforated ribbon. This was the beginning of programming. This invention was perfected in 1728 by his assistant, Jean-Baptiste Falcon, who used a series of interconnected perforated cards. Jacques de Vaucanson took up the idea, replacing the ribbon and cards with a perforated metal cylinder. Joseph-Marie Jacquard is often credited with inventing perforated cards, but all he did was perfect and market the automatic loom in the early 19th century.

In 1833, Charles Babbage described his analytical machine. It was a programmable mechanical calculator using punched cards as data and powered by steam. Although his theory was correct, the lack of sufficiently precise mechanical parts and public funding prevented the machine from being built. Ada Lovelace created a series of programs (a sequence of punched cards) for this machine, and her efforts made her the world'.s first programmer

On the advice of Herman Hollerith (who went on to create IBM), the *United States Census Bureau* used perforated cards for the 1890 census.

In the nineteenth and twentieth centuries, electricity made it possible to motorise mechanical calculators and replace certain mechanisms with electromechanics.

CHAPTER II

COMPUTER

11.1. DEFINITION

From the Latin *ordinator,* one who puts things in order, from *ordinare*. Automatic machine for processing information, obeying programmes formed by sequences of arithmetical and logical operations.

11.2. ADVANTAGE

- **Increased productivity and efficiency**: One of the advantages of a computer is that it can significantly increase productivity and efficiency by automating repetitive tasks, enabling rapid multi-tasking and easy access to information, and facilitating collaboration with others. For example, word processing programmes can make it easier to write and edit documents, spreadsheets can help analyse and organise data, and communication tools such as email and instant messaging can facilitate fast and effective communication.
- **Improved communication and collaboration**: Computers and the internet have made it easier for people to communicate and collaborate with others, regardless of distance. Applications such as email, instant messaging, videoconferencing instant messaging, videoconferencing and tools
collaboration such as Google Docs, Trello and Asana
enable team members to work together on projects in real time, thanks to technological communication.
- **Access to vast amounts of information**: The internet provides us with an almost limitless amount of information, allowing us to learn and research almost any topic imaginable. This is beneficial for both personal and professional reasons, enabling individuals and organisations to stay informed and make better decisions.
- **Automating repetitive tasks**: Computers can be programmed to automate repetitive tasks, saving time and reducing errors. For example, a computer can automatically calculate the salaries of all the employees in an organisation, or automatically send e-mails to customers in a particular database.

The ability to work remotely: Thanks to computers and the internet, employees can now work remotely. This allows them to work from anywhere and increase the flexibility of their work-life balance, including using the best laptops for entrepreneurs. This can be particularly useful for people with children or other family responsibilities that make it difficult to work traditional 9 to 5 office hours.

11.3. COMPUTER GENERATION

The history of the computer dates back to the 1930s with the invention of the Turing machine, considered to be the first computer. However, it was the ENIAC (Electronic Numerical Integrator And Computer) that really marked the beginning of the computer age in 1946. This gigantic machine was capable of performing calculations in a matter of seconds, which represented a revolution for the time.

The first generation of computers, from 1945 to 1955, was characterised by the use of electronic tubes to process information. Computers of this era were very expensive, bulky and unreliable.

The second generation of computers, which lasted from 1956 to 1964, marked the arrival of transistors. These electronic components made it possible to miniaturise computers and reduce production costs. Computers of this era were more reliable, faster and cheaper.

The third generation of computers, from 1964 to 1971, was marked by the use of integrated circuits. These electronic components made it possible to further miniaturise computers and increase their computing power.

The fourth generation of computers, from 1971 to the present day, is marked by the use of microprocessors. These electronic components made it possible to make computers extremely miniaturised and provide even greater computing power. Computers then became accessible to the general public.

Finally, the fifth generation of computers, which is currently being developed, is marked by the use of artificial intelligence and quantum computers. These ultra-powerful computers are capable of solving complex problems in record time.

The different generations of computing can be divided into three main periods: the era of mechanisation (before 1945), the era of electronics (1945-1975) and the era of personal computing (since 1975).

In conclusion, the first computer was created in 1946 by J. Presper Eckert and John Mauchly, and since then the computer has undergone a dazzling evolution. The 5 generations of the computer have seen it evolve from a gigantic, expensive machine into an ultra-powerful tool that is accessible to everyone. Technology continues to advance, and who knows what the future holds?

11.4. TYPE OF COMPUTER

There have been many different types of computer since the dawn of computing. Here are a few examples of the most commonly used computers today.

1. The desktop computer

This is a personal computer designed to be used on a desktop because the whole system is broken down into several peripherals, which makes it more complicated to move around with it. It is generally made up of :

- a screen
- a box (Tower or Central Unit) containing all the electronic components required for its operation
- a keyboard
- a mouse

It may also have speakers for sound and other peripherals such as webcams, printers, scanners, etc....). Each computer has its own special features. In some computers, the screen is also the central processing unit (the I Mac, for example).

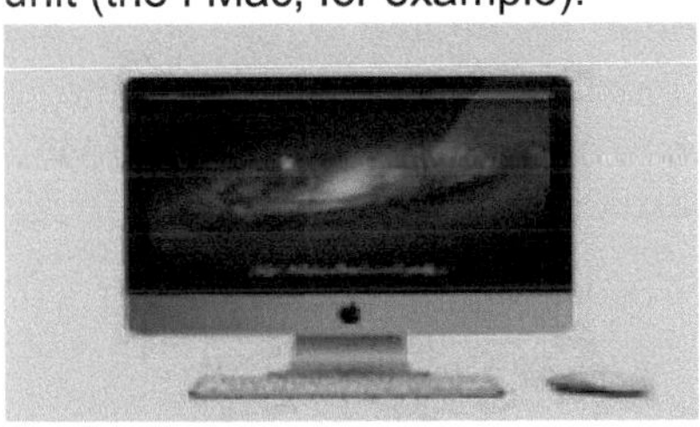

2. The Laptop

It's a personal computer like a desktop. Much smaller, lighter and easier to transport, the laptop is reduced to a single element comprising the usual miniaturised components of a computer:

- The laptop is the box, the central unit containing all the electronic components.
- The integrated screen opens and closes.
- The keyboard is integrated into the case
- A touch-sensitive panel called the "Touchpad" acts as a mouse (an

external mouse can also be connected).

- The laptop has a built-in sound output and also allows headphones to be plugged in.
- Connections and drives are also built into the box.

3. Touch tablets and smartphones

The tablet is an ultra-flat computer that is even lighter and smaller than a laptop, without a keyboard or mouse (which have been replaced by a touch screen). Other peripherals are often connected wirelessly or via side connectors. Everything is compressed and miniaturised into a screen that the system software can use to operate the tablet computer.

The smartphone, originally a mobile phone, has become a small computer similar to a small tablet, also using a touch screen.

4. **Games Console**

The console is not really a computer. Primarily designed for video games, the various consoles have few applications other than their entertainment aspects. However, with today's digital and technological developments, some home consoles have functions that are very similar to those of a computer.

- The console is limited to gaming capabilities but has the same components as a desktop computer (processors, graphics card, sound card, drive, etc.).
- The console generally has no keyboard or mouse, only joysticks. But the systems that 'run' the machine often offer virtual keyboard solutions (as with tablets) that appear on the screen.
- The console is designed to be plugged into a Television (or PC). screen capable of receiving connections).
- Today, the console can be connected to the Internet (which makes it very easy to use).

This means that you can communicate online with other people, thanks to a range of optional audio and video peripherals.

II.5.COMPUTER ARCHITECTURE

To process information, a microprocessor alone is not enough; it must be integrated into a minimum system of programmed information processing. John Von Neumann developed a model of a universal machine for programmed information processing (1946). This architecture serves as the basis for most of today's microprocessor systems. It is made up of the following elements: - a central processing unit ;

- a main memory ;
- input/output interfaces

The various components of the system are linked by communication channels known as buses.

1. THE CENTRAL UNIT

It is made up of the microprocessor, which is responsible for interpreting and executing the instructions in a programme, reading or saving the results in the memory and communicating with the exchange units. All the microprocessor's activities are timed by a clock.

The microprocessor is characterised by :

- its clock frequency: in MHz or GHz ;
- the number of instructions per second it is capable of executing; - the size of the data it is capable of processing: in bits. the size of the data it is capable of processing: in bits.

2. THE MAIN MEMORY

It contains the instructions for the program(s) being run and the data associated with this program. Physically, it can often be broken down into :

- a read-only memory (**ROM**) responsible for storing the programme. This is a read-only memory;
- Random Access Memory (**RAM**) for storing intermediate data or the results of calculations. Data can be read or written into it, but is lost when the system is switched off.

Note: Hard disks, floppy disks, CDROMs, etc. are storage devices and are considered as secondary memories.

3. INPUT/OUTPUT INTERFACES

They enable communication between the microprocessor and the peripherals. (Sensor, keyboard, monitor or display, printer, modem, etc.).

A. HARDWARE

In French, the word **hardware** literally translates as materiel. However, it is used in a much more specific way, since it is actually limited to the hardware itself.

Here we are talking about physical equipment, components that are used in computer technology. It is therefore very important to distinguish between hardware and software. These are two complementary elements, but they encompass completely different realities.

1. Central unit

The central processing unit is the case that contains all the electronic hardware needed for a computer to function properly. That said, the keyboard, mouse and screen are strictly connected to it. For example, it is into the computer's central unit that a disk is inserted. However, central units were not designed for laptops, as all the electronic equipment is grouped together under the keyboard.

To best express the importance of the central processing unit, remember that it contains the processor (the computer's brain), the hard disk (its memory), the motherboard (its backbone) and finally the power supply (the computer's heart and lungs).

2. Peripherals

A peripheral is any electronic device that can be connected to a computer. Here are a few examples:

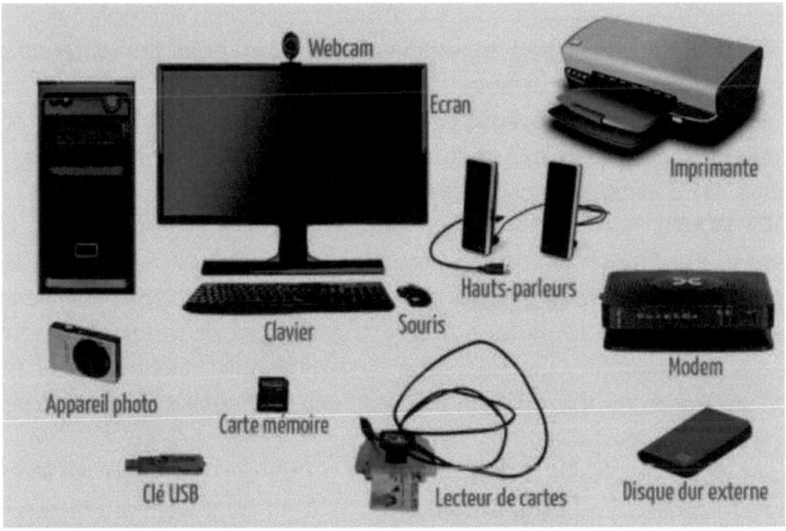

A **screen** displays the contents of the computer.

A **keyboard** and mouse are essential for communicating with the computer.

Loudspeakers are available for listening to sound files. Some screens have built-in speakers.

A **webcam** is a small camera that can be placed on a computer to film images and transfer them to the computer. It can also be integrated into the computer screen.

A **printer** is used to print files on paper. Some printers also have a **"scanner"** function that converts a "paper" page into a computer-readable file.

A **modem**: is a small box used to connect to the Internet.

An **external hard drive**: is a hard drive in a sturdy case that connects to a computer via USB. It can be used to back up data from your computer or to record larger files (films) and transport them.

A **USB flash drive** and a memory card: for storing data on a small, portable device. Memory cards are generally designed for use in cameras, smartphones, etc.

The **card reader:** enables a computer to read information contained on cards: identity cards, memory cards.

CLASSIFICATION OF PERIPHERALS

Peripherals are often divided into 2 categories:

. **Input peripherals**: used to supply information (or data) to the computer system. Examples: keyboard, mouse, scanner, webcam, microphone.

. **Output peripherals**: used to output information from the computer system. Examples: screen, printer, headphones.

There are also **input and output peripherals**, which allow information to be supplied to, but also information to be output from, the computer. Examples: USB stick, memory card, modem, etc.

B. SOFT WARE

Software is the French word for software. Unlike hardware, **software is not tangible, but it does enable the computer to function**. Software enables the computer to perform a very specific task depending on how it is used. For example, the operating system enables the computer to function and process the data on the machine. Otherwise, you can't do anything with the hardware.

Software does not have a lifetime. You can always use them as long as they are operational on the market or as long as their manufacturer authorises their circulation. For example, you can still have the XP operating system. The only drawback is that you will be limited in terms of functionality. **Software that is no longer functional is said to be "obsolete"**.

Also, **software cannot lose performance and power during use**. They are simply updated each time a new version is released on the market. So the only factor that can vary the price of software with the same model and the same manufacturer is the version alone.

THE DIFFERENT TYPES OF SOFTWARE

There are in fact different kinds of Software depending on how it interacts:

- application software used to perform a specific task,
- standard software designed to be given to customers,
- specific software designed for a particular customer,
- open-source software.

BASIC SOFTWARE (Operating system*)*

An **operating system**, or OS, defines a set of programs responsible for establishing a relationship between the various hardware resources, applications and the user.

In a computer, the **operating system** has several missions. Among other things, it manages the processor and RAM, optimises the execution of applications by allocating the necessary resources to them, provides a certain amount of information on how well the computer is working, etc. It enables peripherals to be used under optimum conditions and protects access to resources. It enables peripherals to be used under optimum conditions and protects access to resources.

An **operating system** usually consists of a kernel, a shell and a file system. In the early 80s, Microsoft introduced windows with 'Windows'.

Among the most widely used **operating systems in** the world today are Apple's Mac OS, Microsoft's Windows and Android for mobile phones and smartphones.

CHAPTER III

MS-DOS

111.1. DEFINITION

MS-DOS is the abbreviation for *Microsoft Disk Operating System*, an operating system launched in July 1981 by Microsoft and based on 86-DOS. DOS is a command-line operating system, unlike today's graphical user interfaces (GUIs). IBM's PC-DOS and Microsoft's MS-DOS, two almost identical systems, ran PCs from the 1980s until the mid-1990s, before being replaced by Windows .[2]

111.2. STUDY OF SOME ORDERS

Since version 5, Microsoft has provided brief help on DOS commands. To do this, type the command name. There is a whole range of commands in DOS. But in this section, we are going to present ten of the most commonly used DOS commands, which are listed in the table below, along with the names and details of each command.

№	BACK CONTROL	DESIGNATION AND DETAILS OF THE ORDER
1	CLS	**Clear screen**: here the command is used on its own, with no option
2	HELP	**Get help with MS-DOS commands**. also have the command **command_name/?** or **help command_name** to get help a special order. Example : -help cd or -cd/ ? produce the same result as the **CD** command help.
3	COPY	Copies one or more files to another location. You must first specify the name of the source file and the path to the target. The syntax is: **COPY** file_name.extension path to target
		Example: d:\Copy management.pdf c:\mes files You can also use the **copy *.* d** command, which copies all the files and directories and places them on disk D. You can also use the **MOVE** command with the same parameters.

[2] https://www.futura-sciences.com, consulted on 09/11/2013 at 00h56'

4	DATE	Allows you to view the current date (day / month / year) and modify it.
5	DEL	Used to delete one or more files. The syntax is: **DEL** *names of files or directories to delete*. There are options for this command (/P /F /S /Q /A). Another variant of this command is **ERASE** *names of files or directories to delete* or **RD** *folder_name/S* for deleting directories.
6	DIR	Displays the list of files and sub-directories in a directory. Position the cursor on the current directory and type the command **DIR.**or then type **DIR** *directory_name* wherever the directory is located. Options on file attributes can be found in the help file
7	EXIT	Exits the command interpreter (CMD.EXE). there is also for this ordering options.
8	FIND	Used to search for a string of characters in one or more files. Syntax: FIND search string If possible, you can specify the drive or disk on which the search word might be found, indicating the . Display are provided.
9	FORMAT	Used to format a disk for use with Windows 2000. Syntax: FORMAT volume (obviously with options) where volume means the letter of the drive or disk followed by **(:)**. Example **FORMAT** g : (for disk g)
10	RENAME	Renames one or more files or directories. Syntax .**RENAME** [drive or disk] [path] old_file_name new_file_name. The **REN** command plays the same role as **RENAME**. In fact, it's an abbreviation of RENAME.

NB: to say that these commands are the most widely used is subjective, because not all of them are. It all depends on who uses them and for what purpose. However, the other commands (more commonly used or not) can be obtained from the HELP command in the command prompt.

111.3. MS DOS FILE AND FOLDER MANAGEMENT

The data stored on the disk is in the form of documents called "files". Initially, the word file meant "collection of files". For the uninitiated, the term is confusing because in computing the word file is used to designate a SINGLE document. "File" and "Document" are synonyms here. Documents are grouped together in directories, also known as folders.

These are organised in a hierarchical tree structure. Each directory can contain other directories which in turn can contain other directories.

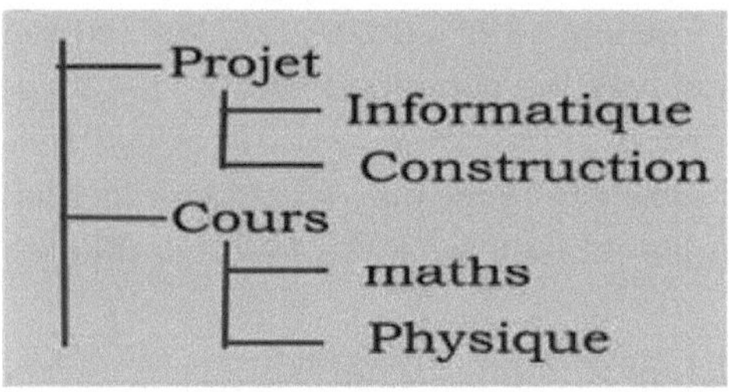

111.3.1. FILE AND DIRECTORY NAMES

Files and directories have names which, in the days of DOS, had the 8.3 format: eight characters followed by a full stop and a maximum of three extension characters. These restrictions have disappeared since Windows 95. Spaces are even allowed in names, which can now be long, but these spaces are still misinterpreted by DOS commands. by DOS commands.

The root directory, the one at the base of the disk, doesn't really have a name. It is designated by the back-slash character '\'. The full name of a file is its name preceded by the full path that allows it to be found from the root directory.

Example :

C:\Cours\OS\Chap1.txt

111.3.2. FILE ATTRIBUTES

Attributes are pieces of information that are stored with the file name.

R read only	Read only. Protected against modification
H hidden	Cache or more accurately "mask", as it is still possible to request their display. (DIR /a)
S system	Attribute reserved for certain sensitive files
A archive	Attribute for organising backups.

This attribute is set as soon as the file is modified. The backup commands can be deleted as soon as the backup is complete.

These attributes are visible under Windows in the file properties, which can be accessed by right-clicking on the file name, then choosing "Properties" from the context menu.

III.3.3.DIRECTORY OPERATIONS

The most important commands for directories are :

MD (Make Directory);PATH; CD (Current Directory), JOIN;TREE; DELTREE (Delete tree); SUBST; CHDIR; MOVE; XCOPY.

1. ACCESSING DIRECTORIES

To access a directory or sub-directory, simply type the command "CD" or "CHDIR" followed by the name of the target directory or sub-directory.

Syntax: **C:\>CD[Target directory name]**

The prompt becomes: **C:\ [Name of current directory]>.**

If you want to access subdirectories, you must either access the parent directory through to the child directories, step by step, by executing the CD command with the above syntax, or access the child directories directly by typing all the directories (parent directory, intermediate subdirectories and the target subdirectory) on a single command line as follows:

C :\>CD\[Father directory name]\[Subdirectory name]\[Name target subdirectory]

To move from a current directory to the parent directory, :

C:\[Current directory name]>CD...

If you are in subdirectories and want to leave them to go directly to the root directory of the hard disk or floppy disk, simply type the following command:

C:\[Current directory/subdirectory]>CD

To go from one directory to another without going through the root directory, type the command as follows:

C:\[Current directory name]>CD\[Target directory name]

2. DISPLAY DIRECTORY CONTENTS AND THEIR ARBORESCENCE

To display the contents of a directory, use the "DIR" command and its switches. On the other hand, to view the tree structure of a directory, use the "TREE" command and its switches.

2.1. The DIR command

To display the contents of the root directory of a hard disk, type the command as follows:

C:\>DIR

The /P switch allows you to display the list of files and directories screen

by screen by pressing any key on the keyboard.
C:\>DIR/P

The /W switch is used to display the full width of the screen in five columns.
C:\>DIR/W

2.2. The TREE command

To obtain the directory tree, use the command
TREE.

The root directory tree of the hard disk is created by typing :

C:\>TREE

And to display it screen by screen, type the command as follows:

C:\>TREE |MORE

3. CREATING A DIRECTORY

Directories are created using the "MD" or "MKDIR" command with the following syntax:

C:\>MD [Directory Name]

Creating a subdirectory is done in the same way as for a directory, just make the prompt in the current directory where you want to insert a subdirectory.

Here are some examples:

The MUSICAL directory on the hard disk (as on a floppy disk) is created as follows:

C:\>MD MUSICAL

To create sub-directories, for example CLASSIC and JAZZ, in the MUSICAL directory, you must first access it by typing :

C:\>CD MUSICAL

Then create the sub-directories one by one as follows: C:\MUSICAL>MD CLASSIC Then C:\MUSICAL>MD JAZZ

To access one of these sub-directories, simply type the CD command from the current MUSICAL directory, as described above.

4. DELETING OR ERASING A DIRECTORY

A directory can only be deleted from the directly ascending parent directory.

The RD command can only delete a directory if its child directories and all its files are deleted first.

Syntax: C:\>RD [Directory name]

The DELTREE command deletes directories, subdirectories and all files. This is why it is followed, after execution, by a deletion confirmation message. The DELTREE command can also be used to delete all the directories on a disk unit, simply type :

C:\>DELTREE *.*

Example: suppose you want to delete a subdirectory of MUSICAL, for example, CLASSIC. You must, of course, be in the current MUSICAL directory.

Then type the command as follows:

C:\MUSICAL>DELTREE CLASSIC

Use the RD command to access the CLASSIC sub-directory and delete all its files. You will then need to return to the parent directory, MUSICAL, to delete the CLASSIC sub-directory:

C:\MUSICAL>RD CLASSIC

5. RENAME A DIRECTORY

A directory can only be renamed from the parent directory. To rename a directory or sub-directory, use the MOVE command followed by the name of the directory to be changed and the new name required.

The syntax is as follows:

C:\>MOVE [Old directory name] [New directory name]

Example:

To rename the MUSICAL directory to MUSIC, type the command, from the root directory, as follows :

C:\>MOVE MUSICAL MUSIC

However, there is another way of renaming a directory. After the MOVE command, use the disk unit and destination of the old name followed by the disk unit and destination of the new directory name, respecting the concordance.

Example:

To rename the CLASSIC directory in the MUSICAL main directory to CLASIC, with the current prompt being that of the root directory, type :

C:\>MOVE C:\MUSICAL\CLASSIC C:\MUSICAL\CLASIC

III.3.4. THE DIFFERENT COMMANDS ON FILES

The commands relating to files are :

ATTRIB ; COMP ;COPY ; DEL ; DIR ;ERASE, EXE2BIN;EXPAND;FC;FIND,MOVE; MSBACKUP; PATH; PRINT; REN; RENAME; REPLACE; RESTORE; SYS; TYPE; XCOPY.

N.B: There is no command for creating files under MS-DOS. However, MS-DOS does have a text editor which allows files containing text to be created. Files can only be created using software (word processing, programming language, etc.).

How do I display disk unit files?

To display the files contained in the disk drives, you need to use the DIR command and its switches.

Syntax**: C:\>DIR[switch] [Unite disk]:**

Example:

To display the file contents of a diskette's root directory and its parent directories, if any, place the target diskette in the drive and type:

C:\>DIR A: Or under the A: prompt, type : C:\>A: then: A:\>DIR

Or, if the diskette contains a lot of files: A:\>DIR/P

Copying files

Copying files means duplicating selected files in another location. Files are copied using the COPY command.

To copy a file, all you need to do is specify its name, extension and the destination , after the name of the COPY command.

Syntax: **C:\>COPY[Nom.extension] [Unite disque]:\ [Destination]**

Example1:

To copy the MOZART.TXT file, located in the Classic sub-directory of Musical on the hard disk, to the "Music" main directory on the floppy disk, type :

C:\MUSICAL\CLASSIC>COPY MOZART.TXT A:\MUSIQUE

Example2 :

To copy the same file, MOZART.TXT, to the root directory of your hard disk, type :

C:\MUSICAL\CLASSIC>COPY MOZART.TXT C:\

How to copy a group of files or all the files in a directory

To copy all the files or a group of files in a directory, use the MS-DOS wildcards with the COPY command following its syntax.

For example:

To copy all the files in the DOS directory to the root directory of the hard disk, type: **C:\DOS>COPY *.* C:**

For example:

To copy files with the .EXE extension from the DOS directory to the root directory directory of a floppy disk, type:

C:\DOS>COPY *.EXE A:

For example:

To copy all the files in the DOS directory whose name begins with "MS" to the root directory of the hard disk, type :

C:\DOS>COPY MS*.* C:\

CHAPTER IV

WINDOWS

IV.1.PRESENTATION (WINDOWS EXPLORER, DESKTOP, WORKSTATION, RECYCLE BIN)

IV.1.1.WINDOWS EXPLORER

Windows *Explorer* is the application used in modern versions of the Windows operating system to display, explore and use files and directories. Windows Explorer, which was originally completely separate from the Internet Explorer , web browserappeared with Windows 95 as a replacement for the old Microsoft Windows [3]file manager .

Windows Explorer has a function for searching for files on the local computer network. Explorer also displays the Microsoft Windows desktop, including the taskbar and Start menu.

Examples of common explorer shortcuts :

- *explorer.exe /e,C:* Displays the contents of the C: drive and the folder explorer pane
- *explorer %WINDIR%*: opens the windows directory directly in windows explorer.
- *explore %USERPROFILE%*: opens the current user's directory directly: (default : *C:\Documents and Settings\%USERNAME%*)
- *(Windows key)* + *E*: opens My Computer directly in Windows Explorer
- *(windows key)* + *D*: collapses all running applications to display the desktop
- *(windows key)* + *R* : launches the dialog box: task execution
- *(windows key)* + *L*: locks the current user session

IV.1.2 OFFICE

The desktop consists of a background image, also known as the "Desktop", the Recycle Bin, File Explorer and various shortcuts (to your programs, files and folders). It gives you quick access to your favourite programs, as well as to your entire computer via Explorer (also known as "My Computer"). Windows offers a wide range of desktop customisation options.

The desktop consists of the ***background,*** the ***icons,*** the ***Start menu*** and the ***taskbar***. Let's take a look at what these elements are used for.

- The **background** allows you to display the image or photo of your choice.

[3] https://www.techno-science.net, consulted on 09/11/2023 at 02h38'

- The **icons** give you access to the essential elements of Windows (the Recycle Bin, File Explorer, etc.), as well as your favourite programs.
- **The taskbar** displays the Start menu, lets you search your computer, displays your favourite programs and open programs, and displays system information via the quick access zone (date, time, internet connection status, battery level, antivirus protection, etc.) and notifications (updates to install, etc.).

A. DESKTOP ICONS

There are several icons on the desktop: the Recycle Bin, Explorer (also called My Computer), and various shortcuts to your favourite programs. To open a program, file or folder on the desktop, double-click its icon.
To create a desktop shortcut to a file or folder, simply do the following: right-click on the file or folder/Send to Desktop (create a shortcut).

B. VIRTUAL DESKTOPS: WORKING WITH SEVERAL DESKTOPS

You can create several desktops in Windows 11, by clicking on the desktop management icon to the right of the search icon on the taskbar. This is useful if you're multitasking or if you use your PC for both personal and professional purposes. You can, for example, create an additional desktop that will only be used for personal tasks.
Note that icons will be displayed in the same way on the different desktops created. However, an application opened on desktop 1 will not be displayed on desktop 2, which is the whole point of virtual desktops. Virtual desktop management also exists in Windows 10.

C. ACCESSING THE DESKTOP FROM THE TASK BAR (Windows 11)

If you are working with several windows open and you want to display the desktop quickly, click on the far right of the taskbar:

D. ADD FOLDERS TO THE DESKTOP

Adding a new folder to your desktop couldn't be easier! **Right-click on the desktop and select New >Folder.** All that's left to do is give it a name and move it where you want.

To create a new folder, select **New->Folder** :

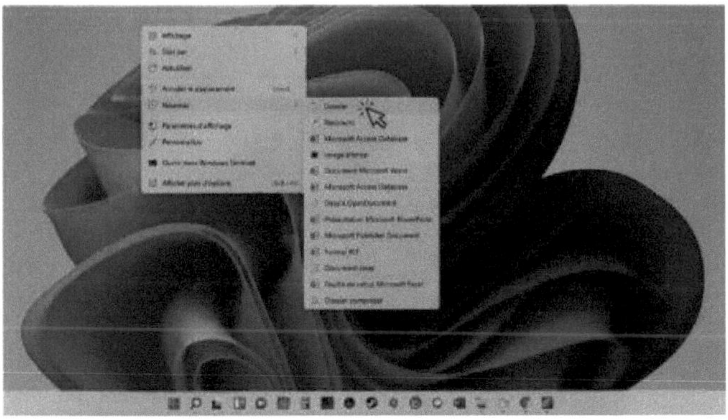

E. ORGANISING, CREATING AND DELETING ICONS

To organise your icons (shortcuts, files or folders on the desktop), **move them by holding down the left mouse button. Release where required.** The moved icon will automatically be aligned "on the invisible grid". Create folders, and move the desired icons into them by dragging the icon onto the folder, then releasing the mouse.

To delete an icon, right-click on it and select "Delete". You can also select an icon by clicking on it once and pressing the "Delete" key on your keyboard.

You can also store files on the desktop, but it's advisable not to clutter it up with files and folders, as this can slow down the computer. On a desktop, the ideal is to keep only shortcuts!

F. CHANGE THE OFFICE IMAGE

To change the desktop background image, **right-click on the desktop and select "Customise". Then click on 'Browse', and select the image or photo you want.** You can then centre or expand the new image using the 'Choose a size' drop-down menu. Let's take a look.

Right-click on **'Customise'**:

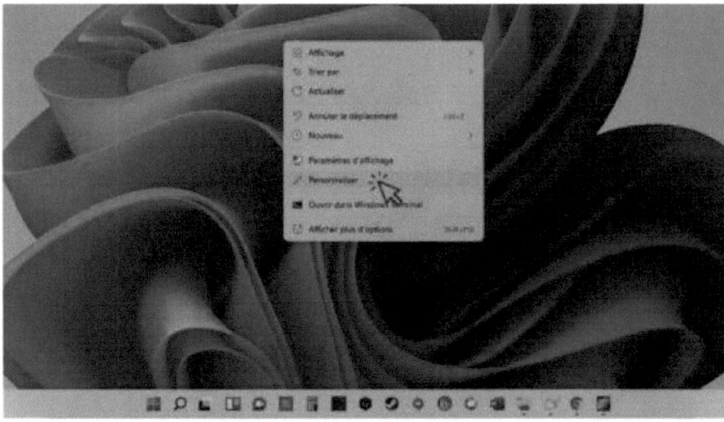

Then click on "**Background**":

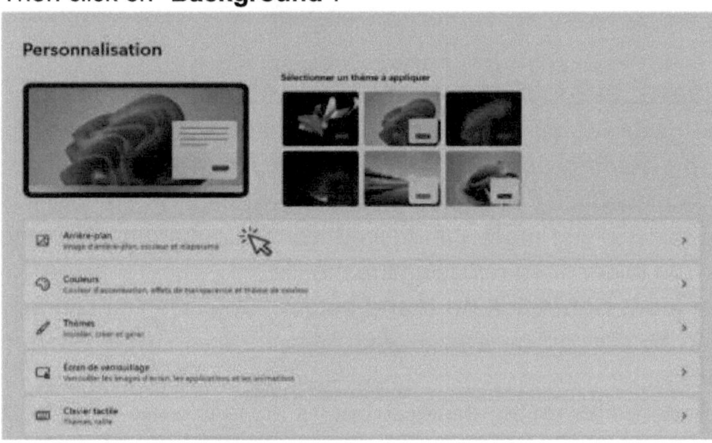

Finally, click on "**Browse photos**" to select the photo of your choice:

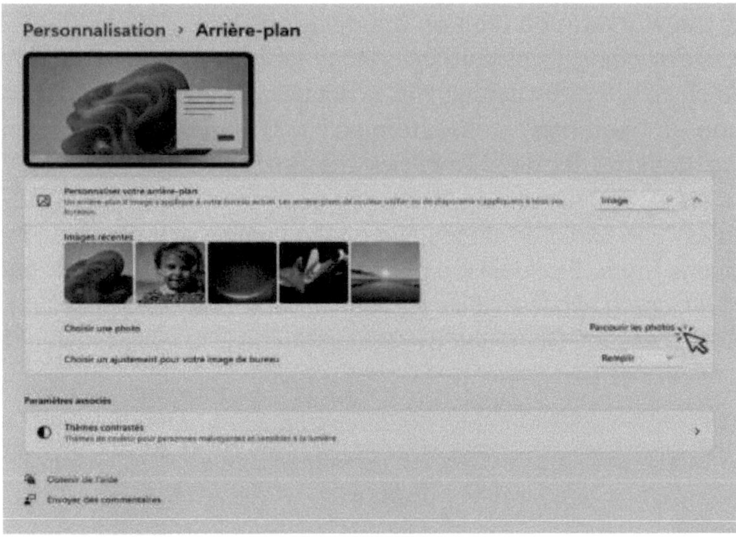

Another way to change your desktop **background** is to go to the folder of your choice in Explorer, for example the "My Pictures" folder, and right-click on the photo you want. Then choose **"Choose as desktop background".**

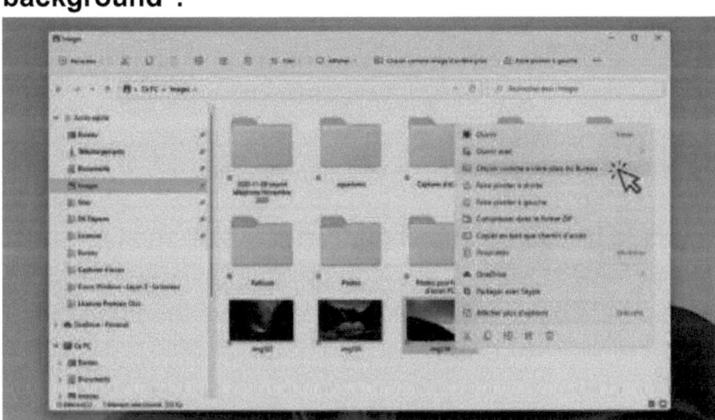

The new back-plan is now in place!

IV.1.3.WORKSTATION (FILE EXPLORER)

A workstation provides access to all the files on a computer. It also provides access to all branch drives and peripherals: hard disk, external hard disk, CD/DVD drive, USB key, SD card, smartphone, etc.

It also lets you manage all your files: move, copy, delete, rename, search and sort them.

1. WORKSTATION PRESENTATION

A. Display the workstation icon on the desktop

First of all, we're going to display this handy icon that lets you quickly access files on your PC. By default, this is not present in Windows. Go to **"Start menu" / "Settings" / "Customise" / "Theme"** then click on **"Customise desktop icons"**. Then tick the box corresponding to My Computer, "This PC".

Also known as "File Explorer" depending on the version of Windows, File Explorer opens from the desktop. **Double-click "This PC" or "My Computer"** to open Windows File Explorer. If you don't see this icon, you can also access My Computer by clicking on the little yellow folder at the bottom of your screen.

B. There are two main areas in File Explorer: the side menu, on the left, which shows your folder tree and lets you quickly navigate to a drive or folder, and the display area, on the right, which shows the contents of a drive or folder:

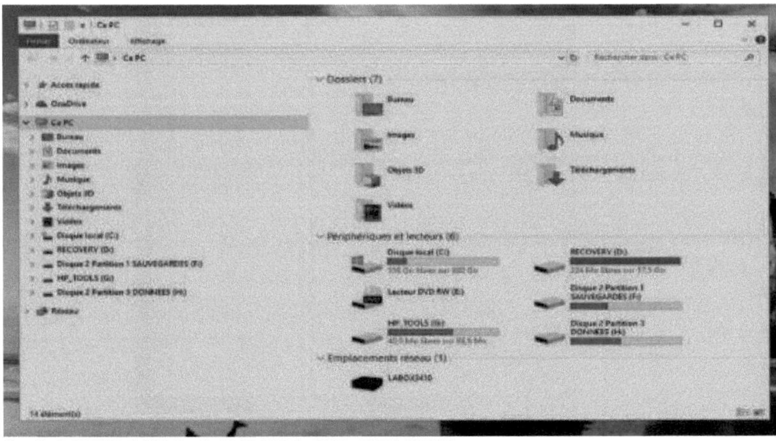

2. ACCESSING A DRIVE OR DEVICE

In the side navigation menu, **click on "This PC"** to display all the drives and peripherals connected to your computer (USB stick, SD card, external hard drive, etc.). **Then double-click on the drive of your choice** to display its contents. You can also use only the left-hand side menu to
browse **folders.**

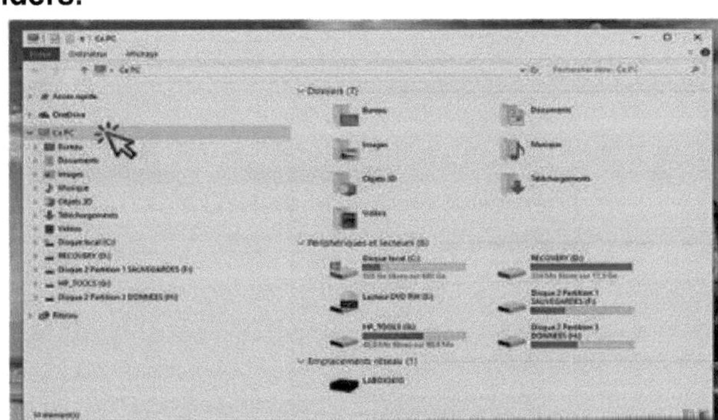

3. ACCESSING FILES AND FOLDERS

There are two ways of accessing files and folders. You can reach your target folder **by double-clicking on your drives and folders**, or you can **use the lateral menu tree**, as shown below.
In this example, we're going to display the folders on "Disk C:" using the lateral menu. **Click on "This PC"** on the left-hand side of Explorer:

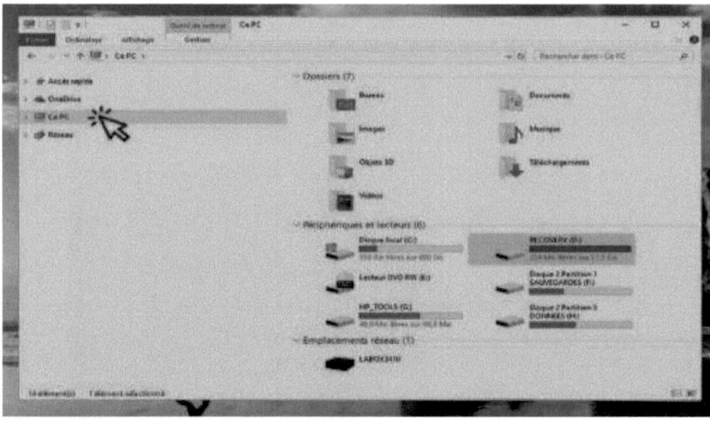

The computer tree then unfolds:

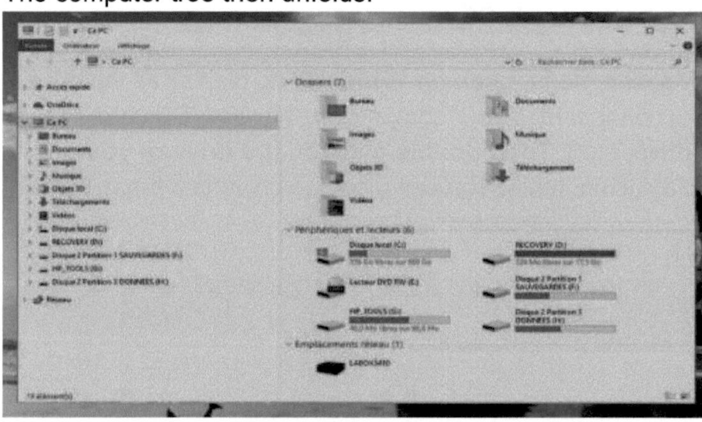

Then click on "Local disk (C:)". :

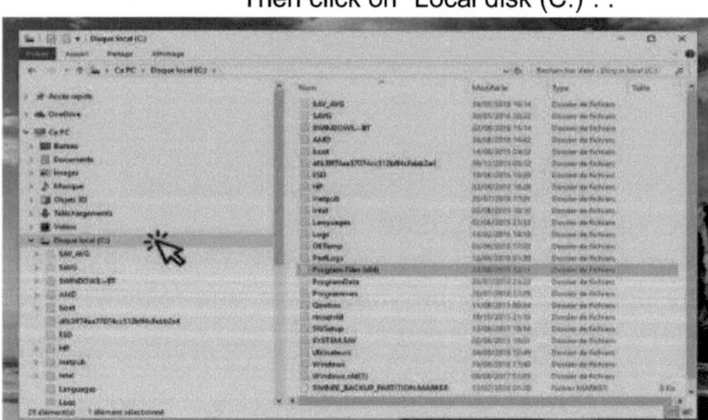

And deploy the folders until you reach the folder of your choice. Its contents will then be displayed on the right-hand side of Explorer.

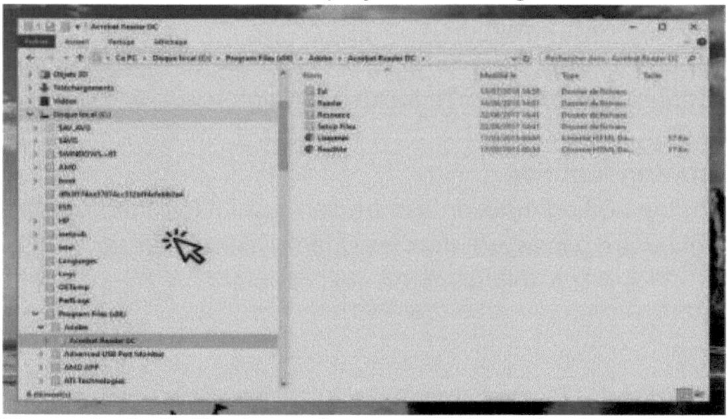

To navigate in Explorer, for example to go backwards, use the 2 navigation arrows at the top left of your window:

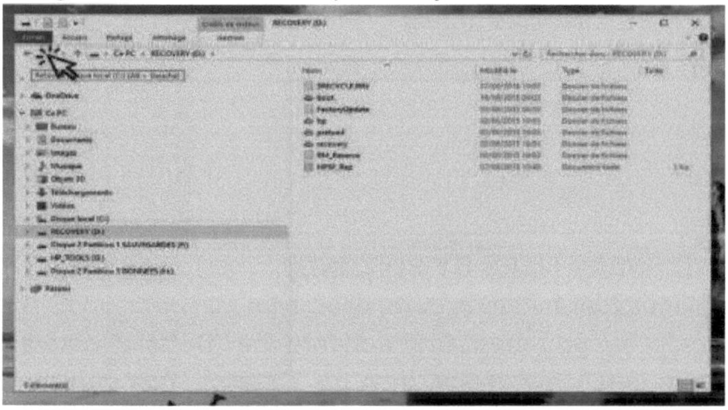

It's easy to **access your "personal folders"** from File Explorer, **because these folders are directly accessible from the side menu: "Documents, "Pictures", "Music", "Downloads".** Also look out for the "**Quick Access"** tab at the top of your side navigation menu, which gives you quick access to recently opened folders.

4. SEARCH FOR FILES ON YOUR COMPUTER

To find a file or folder on your computer, Explorer has a search function at the top right of the window. **Enter the name of the file you want to search for in the search field and Windows will automatically find the file**.

A. Display all files of the same type

If you want to search for all files of the same type, enter *.filetype

Examples: to display all the MP3 files on your computer, type *.mp3 To display all the photos and images, type *.jpg

B. Display a file's parent folder

You've found your file and want to access its folder? To access the parent folder containing the file you're looking for, right-click -> "Open file location" on the file.

C. Using the sorting function

During a search, the sorting function can be very useful for changing the way the items found are displayed, thus making the search easier.

This is the subject of the next chapter.

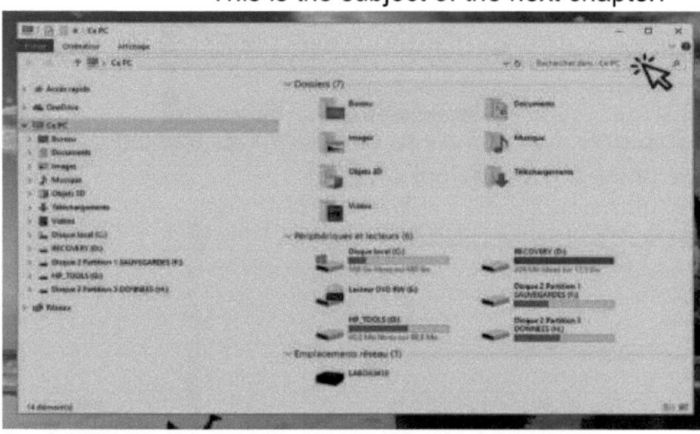

5. SORT FILES (DISPLAY FILES BY SORTING)

You can sort files in a folder by name, size, date, type, etc.

To use the sorting option, **you must first activate the "Details" display mode** by clicking on the "View" menu, then on "Details". **You can now sort your files by clicking on the desired tab**. For example, click once on the 'Name' tab and all your files will be displayed in alphabetical order. **To change the sorting order, click the tab a second time**.

You can also sort your files and folders using the
Sort by" menu next to the display modes (click on "View" first to access the sorting icon).

Let's take a look. **Click on "Details"** in the menu
"Display:

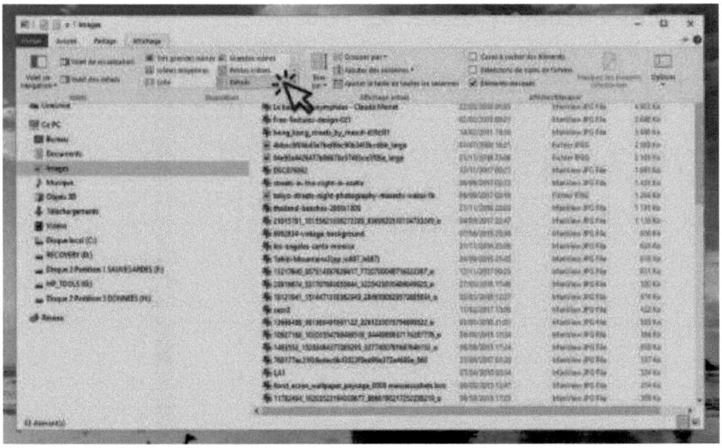

Then click on the desire tab. Here, we have sorted by size :

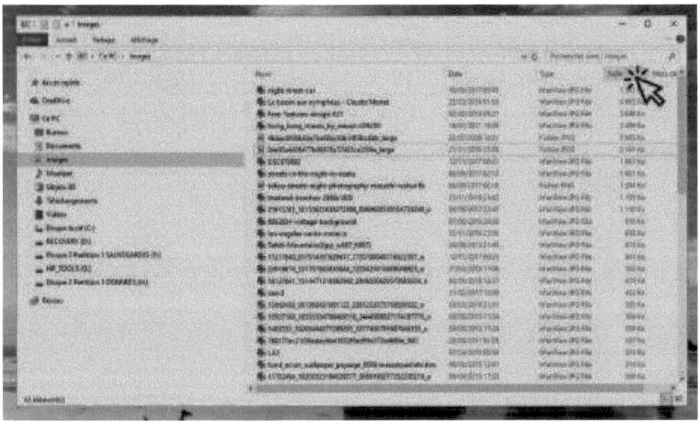

You can also access the sorting function **via the "View" menu**:

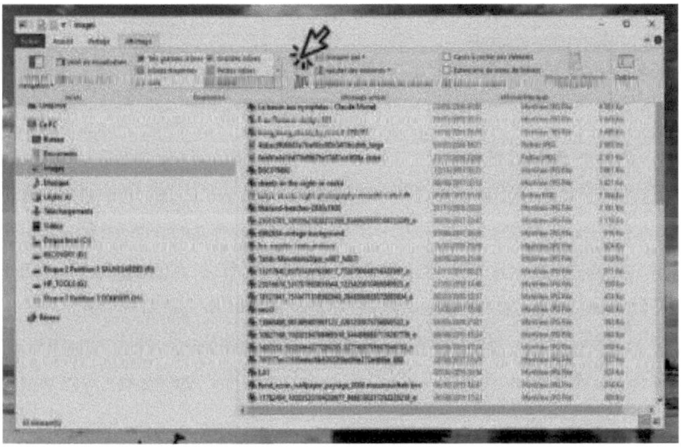

To **access the found element folder**, right-click on the :

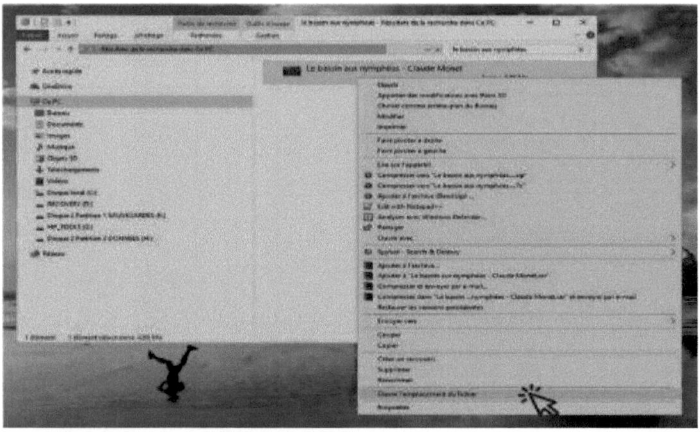

6. POSSIBLE OPERATIONS ON FILES AND FOLDERS

Let's list the main operations that can be performed on files and folders. They are almost all accessible using the context menu (right-click on a file or folder), but can also be used using keyboard shortcuts (see the Cut-Copy-Paste)tab.

- Move
- Copy
- Delete
- Rename
- Create a shortcut
- Send to a device
- Compress
- Print

The context menu can also be used inside the window, **for example to add a new folder: "Right-click > "New"-> "Folder"**. See Creating and organising folders for more information!

A. MOVING A FILE OR FOLDER

To move a file from Explorer, click on it and hold. Move it to the desired location after preparing the target folder in the left-hand side menu (your target folder must be visible in order to reach it with the mouse). When you are on the target folder, release the click. The file will be moved.

If you want to move a file **to a different drive, Windows will make a copy, not a move**. You will then need to use cut and paste to move your file.

The same applies to the files.

B. CHANGE THE WAY FILES AND FOLDERS ARE DISPLAYED

As we saw earlier, you can change the way files and folders are displayed. **What's the point?** For example, it's nicer to have a thumbnail view of your photos, rather than a list of files, which is less informative.

To change the display of the open folder, **click on the**

Click on "Display" and select the display mode you prefer. Simply move the mouse over a display mode to get an instant preview of the result. You can parameterise each folder with a different display, which is really practical!

You can also use the shortcut **"Ctrl" + Mouse wheel** to change the way files are displayed in your Explorer. To see examples of how to do this in pictures, go to Modifying the display of files and folders course on Windows.

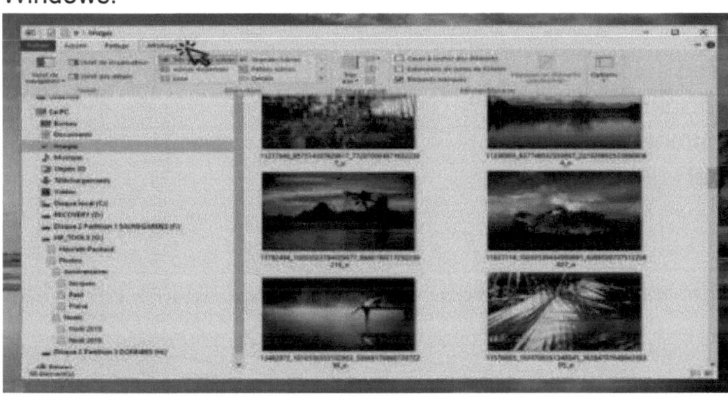

IV.2.APPLICATION SOFTWARE

IV.2.1.DEFINITION

Application software is software designed to solve a specific problem .[4]

IV.2.2.ROLE

Application software is used to manage programs designed for a particular task.

The software **sends the data to the operating system**, which stores it on a medium (the hard disk).

Examples of application software	Specific tasks
Word, Pages, WordPad	Word processing
Excel, Numbers, Quattro Pro	Spreadsheet and spreadsheets

[4] https://www.marche-public.fr, consulted on 09/11/2023 at 02h58'.

	electroniques
PowerPoint, Keynote, CorelFLOW	Presentation, Audio-visual editing
Photoshop, Paint ShopPro, Adobe Illustrator	Image processing
Outlook, Mail, Thunderbird	Email management
Access	Database

IV.2.3.TYPES

Types of application software :

- Word processing software. This software enables users to create and edit documents. ...
- Database software. ...
- Spreadsheets
- Multimedia
- Presentation software
- Enterprise Software
- Software Information Worker
- Educational software.

CHAPTER V

STARTING UP THE COMPUTER

To start up a computer, simply press the Power button located on the computer. Depending on the model, this button may be located on the front, the top or on one side for conventional mainframes. For so-called all-in-one central units, this button can be located on the front, on one side, underneath or even behind the device.

V.1.CONNECTING THE PERIPHERALS TO THE CENTRAL UNIT (see fixed computer)

V.1.1.DEFINITIONS :

A peripheral: A peripheral is a piece of computer hardware that connects to a computer .[5]

A central processing unit: In computing, the central processing unit refers to the case, usually large and rectangular, that comes with a computer. This case contains components that are essential for the computer to function properly .[6]

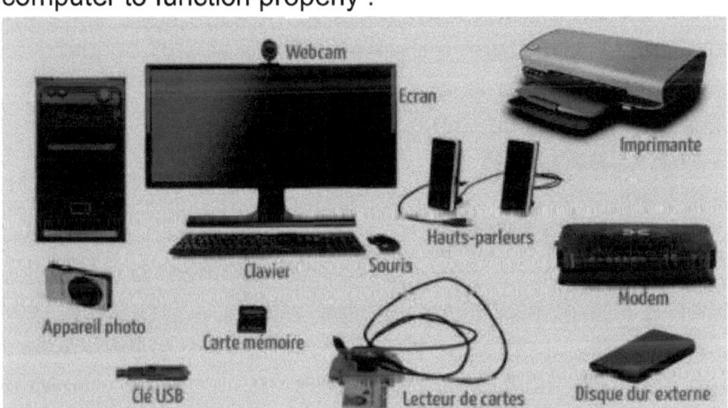

A **screen** displays the contents of the computer.

---

[5] https://cours-informatique-gratuit.fr, consulted on 10/11/2023 at 02:06'.

[6] https://www.futura-sciences.com, consulted on 10/11/2023 at 02:07'.

A **keyboard** and mouse are essential for communicating with the computer.

Loudspeakers are available for listening to sound files. Some screens have built-in speakers.

A **webcam** is a small camera that can be placed on a computer to film images and transfer them to the computer. It can also be integrated into the computer screen.

A **printer** is used to print files on paper. Some printers also have a **"scanner"** function that converts a "paper" page into a computer-readable file.

A **modem** is a small box used to connect to the Internet.

An **external hard drive** is a hard drive in a sturdy enclosure that connects to a computer via USB. It can be used to back up data from your computer or to record larger files (films) and transport them.

A **USB key** and a memory card can be used to store data on a small, portable device. Memory cards are generally designed to be placed in cameras, smartphones, etc.

The **card reader** enables a computer to read information contained on cards, such as ID cards and memory cards.

CLASSIFICATION OF PERIPHERALS

Peripherals are often divided into 2 categories:

. **Input peripherals**: used to supply information (or data) to the computer system. Examples: keyboard, mouse, scanner, webcam, microphone.

. **Output peripherals**: used to output information from the computer system. Examples: screen, printer, headphones.

There are also **input and output peripherals**, which can be used to provide information, but also to output information from the computer. Examples: USB stick, memory card, modem, etc.

V.2. OPENING THE COMPUTER

See how to get started

V.3. LAUNCHING A PROGRAMME

If you want to use a program on your MS-equipped Windows computer, you need to open it first. If you're not familiar with how your computer works or if you've recently updated your operating system to from a very old version, then you may have difficulty locating the program you want to use. Fortunately, there are three very simple steps to finding and opening a program on your computer, which are easy to follow.

1. Go to your **"Start"** button and click on it. It is located at one end of the taskbar. This is the bar that remains on your computer and shows you

your currently open programmes. It may be along the bottom of your screen, at the top of your screen, or along the left or right hand side of your screen.

2. Scroll down to "**All Programs**" and wait for the program menu to pop up. If you have already used the programme, it may also be located somewhere in the line above the 'All Programmes' option. There are usually six to nine recently used programmes found here.

3. Locate the program you want to open and click on it. Depending on where your desired program is saved, you may have to search in the secondary menus. For example, if you want to use the calculator, you'll first need to go to "Accessories", then locate the calculator in the secondary pop-up menu.

V .4.CLOSING A PROGRAM

To close an application on a Windows PC, you can either click on the "X" button in the top right-hand corner of the program window, or use the keyboard shortcut "Alt+F4". When you click on the 'X' button, the program will ask you if you wish to save the changes you have made before closing. If you choose to save, the program will close after the changes have been saved. If you choose not to save, the programme will close immediately.

CLOSING A PROGRAM WITHOUT A MOUSE

If your mouse doesn't work, you can always close an open program using the keyboard. To do this, press 'Alt+Tab' to go to the program you want to close, then press 'Alt+F4' to close it. If you have more than one program open, you can use the 'Tab' key to switch between them.

QUIT ALL OPEN APPLICATIONS ON A PC

If you have several programs open and want to close them all at once, you can use the keyboard shortcut "Ctrl+Alt+Delete". This will bring up the Task Manager, where you can see all the programs running on your PC. To close all open applications, click on "End task" for each program

CLOSING A PROGRAMME THAT HAS STOPPED

If a program has stopped responding or stopped running, you can use the Task Manager to close it. To do this, press "Ctrl+Shift+Esc" to open the Task Manager. Then find the program that has stopped in the "Processes" tab and click "End Task" to close it.

CHAPTER VI

FILE AND DOCUMENT MANAGEMENT IN WINDOWS

VI .1.NOTION OF FILE AND FOLDER

We often talk about files and folders when we use a computer. But these basic terms can seem obscure when you're just starting out in computing, or when your use of a computer is limited to doing a few searches, exchanging messages or watching videos.

What is a file and what is a folder?

A file can be a video, a photo, a piece of music or a document that will be stored on a computer, a USB key, a CD, ... Whatever the location, a file always has a name, an extension and is represented by an icon.

For example, the name of a file will end with a dot followed by 3 letters (the extension). Ex: facture.doc, mont-blanc.jpg, . The file name is chosen by the author when the file is created, but it can be changed without any problem at a later date. On the other hand, an extension is not worth changing because it defines the type of file and the programme/software that will be used to open it.

Text Spreadsheet

PdfMusic Image Film

If you have a file on your computer, you will also need the right software to open and read it, otherwise you will only see the title. You won't be able to read the document, listen to the song or watch the film in your file. Rest assured, most common files can be read by the programmes already installed on your computer.

If you want to compare a file to a real-life object, it would be a letter, a CD, a photo, etc.

A folder is completely different from a file. A folder cannot be read and has no extension.

A folder is used to arrange files so that they can be found more easily. It can also contain sub-folders that contain files.

A file can be compared to a filing cabinet, a , a photo album or a cardboard box.

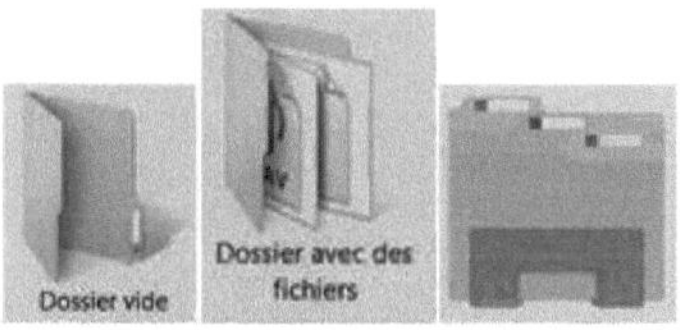

VI.2.CREATING A FILE

There are several ways of creating a folder, but here we will show just one method, that of creating a folder when you save your document using the Save As dialog box.

1. Open your document, then click **on File**> **Save as.**
2. Under **Save As,** select the location where you want to create your folder. You may need to click **Browse or** Computer and navigate to the location of your new folder.
3. In the Save As **dialog box** which opens, click New **folder.**

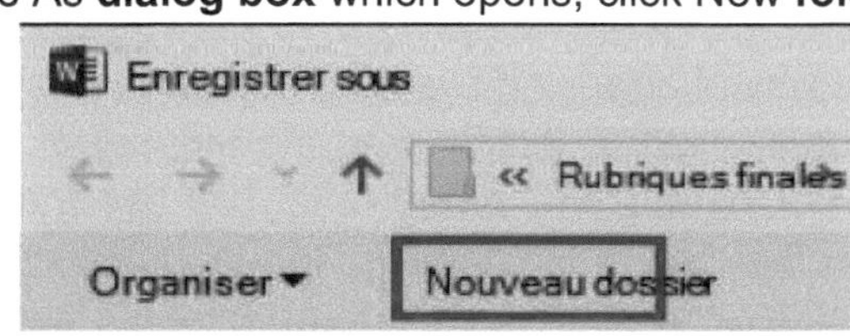

4. Type the name of your new folder, then press Enter.

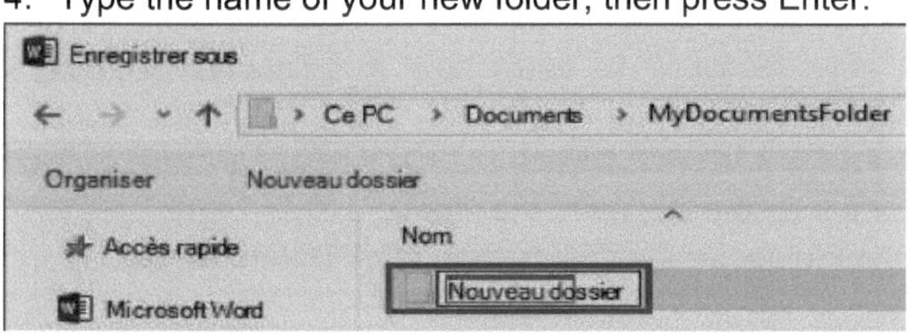

Note: You cannot use slashes, colons, semicolons, dashes or full stops in the name of your folder.

VI.3.COPYING OR MOVING FILES AND FOLDERS

You can copy and move files and folders from different fapons in File Explorer. You can :

1rst method: Select the items you want to copy or move, press or click the Home tab, then press Copy to copy them or Cut to move them. Then open the new location, and press or click Paste.

2th method: Open two File Explorer windows side by side, then drag items from one window to the other. (To open a new File Explorer window, press or click the File tab, then choose Open New Window).

3[(rd]) method: Use the keyboard shortcut Ctrl+C to copy or Ctrl+X to cut, then navigate to the new location and press Ctrl+V to paste.

4th method: Hold down or right-click on the element to be copied or moved, choose Cut or Copy from the context menu, hold down or right-click on the new location, then choose Paste from the context menu.

Advice

- The simplest way of arranging two windows next to each other on the desktop is to use alignment. Simply drag the title bar of one window to the extreme left or right of the screen until you see the outline of the window covering that half of the screen. Repeat this step with the other window on the other side of the screen to arrange the two windows side by side.
- If you copy or move a file or folder in a library, it is stored in the library's default save location. To learn how to customise a library's default save location.

VI.4.DELETING FILES AND FOLDERS

To delete a file or folder, the steps are the same.

1. Right-click on the folder to be deleted, then **click Delete folder.**

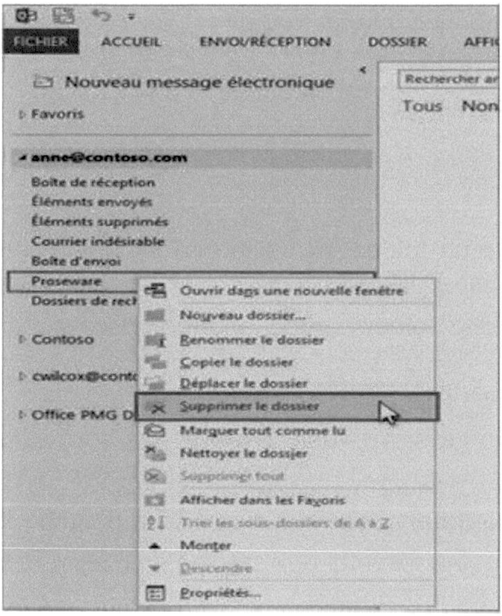
FICHIER
ACCUEIL
ENVOI/RÉCEPTION
DOSSIER
Nouveau message électronique
Favoris
anne@contoso.com
Boîte de réception
Éléments envoyés
Éléments supprimés
Courrier indésirable
Boîte d'envoi
Proseware
Contoso
Office PMG
Tous
Ouvrir dans une nouvelle fenêtre
Nouveau dossier...
Renommer le dossier
Copier le dossier
Déplacer le dossier
Supprimer le dossier
Marquer tout comme lu
Nettoyer le dossier
Supprimer tout
Afficher dans les Favoris
Trier les sous-dossiers de A à Z
Monter
Descendre
Propriétés...

2. **Click** Yes to move the folder and its contents to the **Elements supprimes folder.**

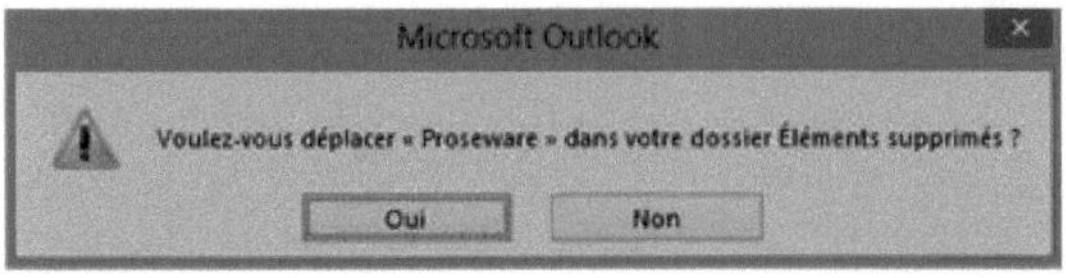

When you empty **the** Deleted Items folder, all its items, including the folders you deleted, are permanently deleted.

Note: You cannot delete embedded folders, such as Inbox, Outbox or **Sent Items.**

VI.5.SEARCHING FOR FILES AND FOLDERS

To search for your files in Windows 10, use one of the following methods.

1. **Perform a search from the taskbar:** Type the name of a document (or a keyword appearing in it) in the search box on the taskbar. The results for the documents on your PC will appear.

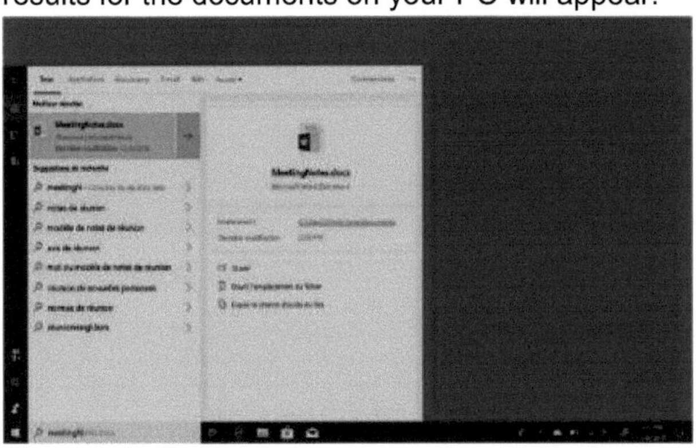

2. **Searching in File Explorer:** Open **File Explorer** from the taskbar or right-click on the **Start** menu, choose **File Explorer**, then select a location in the left pane to search or browse. For example, select **This PC** to search all the devices and drives on your computer, or select **Documents** to search only the files stored there.

VI.6.CHANGING FILE AND FOLDER NAMES

To rename a file or folder :

1. Right-click on the element and choose Rename, or select it and press F2.
2. Write down the new name, then click enter .

You can also change the name of a file in the properties .window

When you rename a file, only the first part of its name is selected, not the extension (the part behind the last .). The extension normally describes the type of file (for example .pdf file is a PDF document) and normally you should not change it. If you still want to change the extension, select the full name and change it.

VI.7.RESTORING DELETED OBJECTS

When you delete a file or folder from your computer, it is actually transferred to the Windows Recycle Bin. **This allows you to recover your file or folder if you make a mistake, for example.** The Recycle Bin is therefore essential, but it needs to be emptied regularly so as not to clutter up your computer unnecessarily!

To recover a deleted file, **double-click to open the Recycle Bin, locate your file and then right-click on "Restore".**

You can restore an accidentally deleted file as long as the Recycle Bin has not been emptied. If, on the other hand, you have unfortunately emptied your Recycle Bin, some specialist programmes are able to recover your files.

Trash is empty, how do I get my files back?

To recover files after accidentally emptying the Recycle Bin, there is recovery software like Recuva that you can download free of charge.

VI.8.DISPLAYING THE CONTENTS OF A FOLDER

To display the contents of a folder, simply :

1. Open **File Explorer** from the taskbar.
2. Select **View> Options> Modify folder and search options**.
3. Select the **View** tab and, in **Advanced settings**,

select **Show cached files, folders and drives**, then **OK**.

VI.9.APPLICATION FOR CREATING FILES AND FOLDERS FOR INCOMING AND OUTGOING ACCOUNTING DOCUMENTS

An accounting file contains all the accounting periods and all the data for a person or company (chart of accounts, entries, addresses, invoices, employees, etc.). There is no limit to the number of accounting folders you can create, as long as you have enough space on your hard disk.

VI.9.1.CREATING AN ACCOUNTING FILE

From the File menu, New Folder, the folder creation wizard opens. Follow the steps in the wizard.

1. In step 1, enter the company details in the Company name tab and and in the Communications tab.

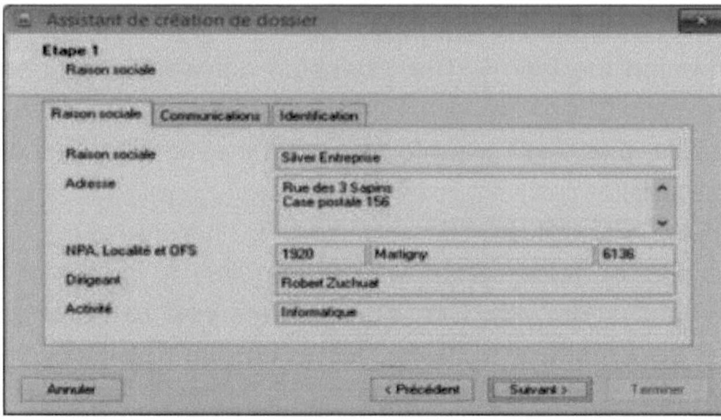

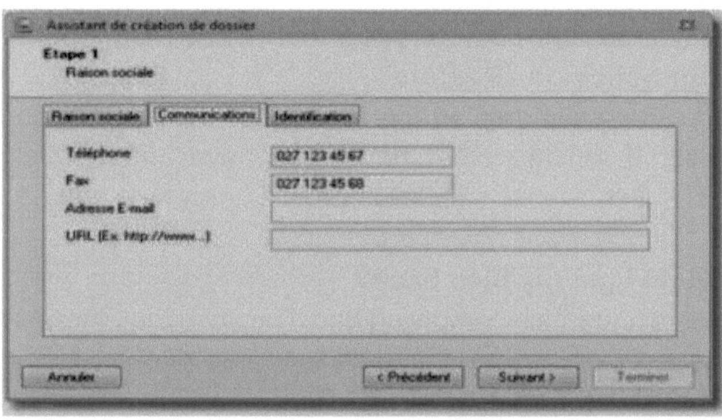

In the Identification tab, enter the IDE number. This field is mandatory for Swissdec accounts. Enter the company's commercial register number, VAT number and AVS number. The file number is entered automatically.

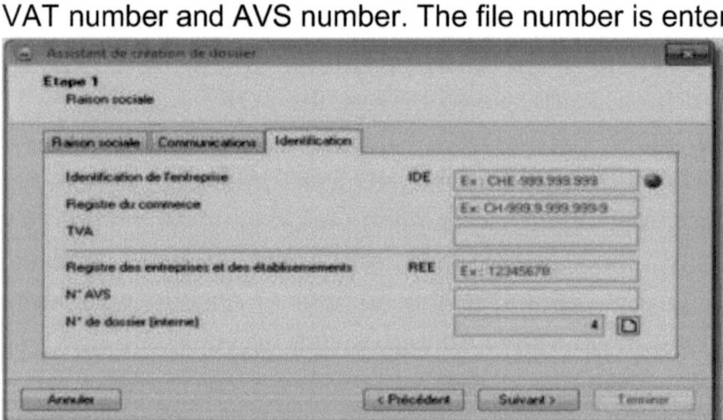

Click on Next

In step 2, determine the dates of the first financial year of this company.

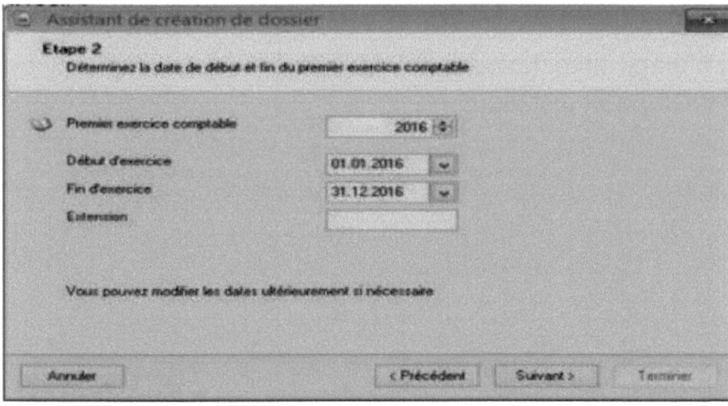

Click on Next

In step 3, select the chart of accounts that will be used in this folder.

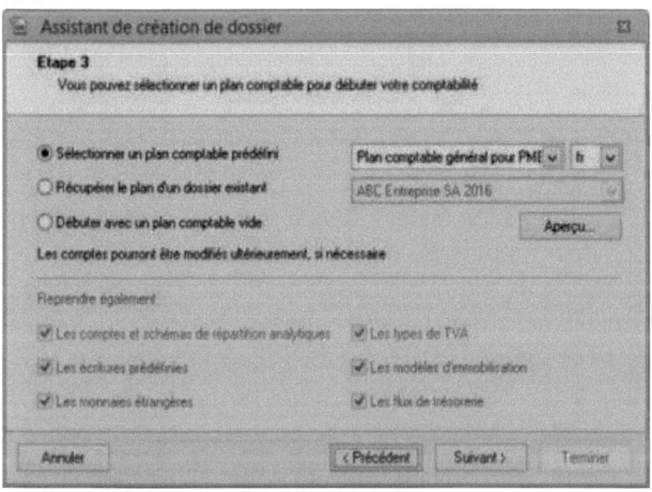

In step 4, determine the VAT details

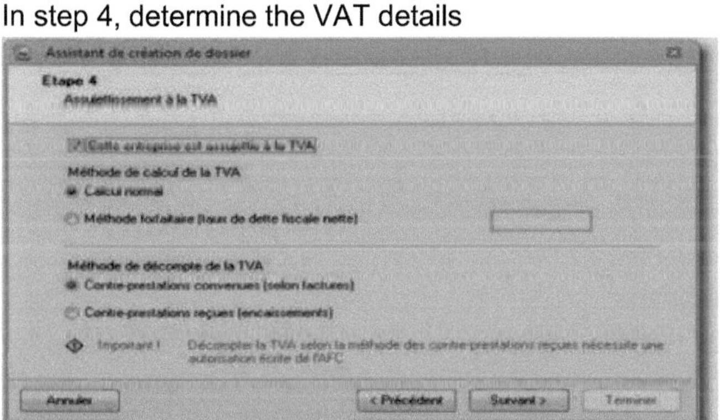

Click on Next

In step 5, select the applications to be activated for the accounting file. You can always change this choice at a later date. Modules can only be activated if they have been installed.

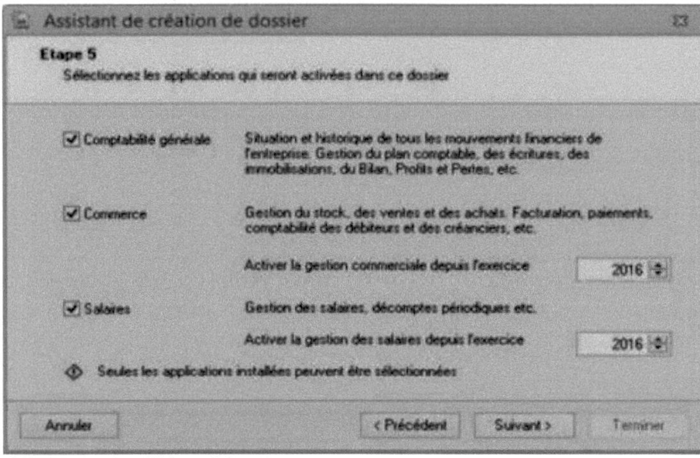

Click on the "Next" button

In step 6, you can choose to start with empty files or automatically define default data.

We advise you to tick the Automatically define data by default option. Winbiz will create payment methods, payment conditions, address and item models. These elements are mainly used in the Commerce module and can then be modified according to your needs.

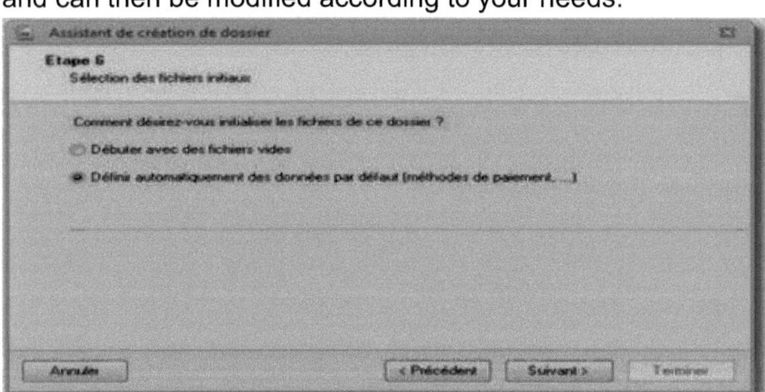

Click on the "Next" button

In step 7, select the order of languages to be used in the forms.

Example of use: In items, you can enter the item description in French, German, English and Italian. If the default language is French, item descriptions will be entered in French by default. A drop-down list allows you to enter descriptions in other languages.

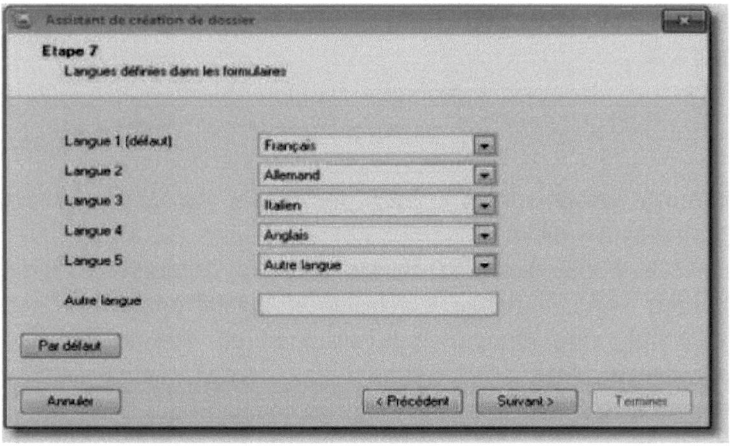

NB: Once the order of the languages has been defined and data has been entered into the software, the order of the languages must not be changed. Click on the "Next" button

In step 8, define the users authorised to view this accounting file.

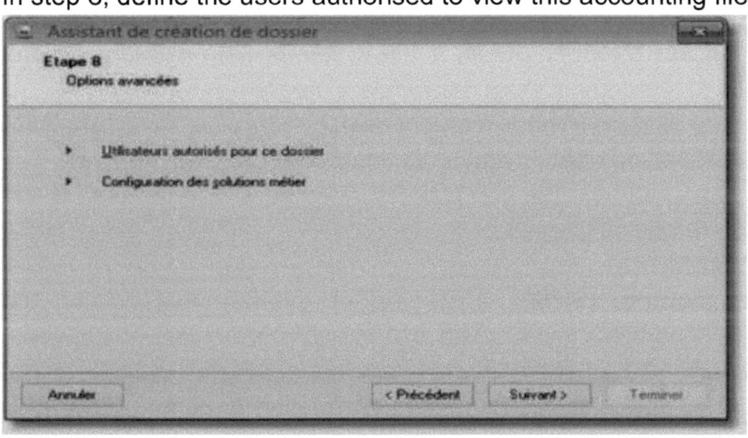

Click on the "Finish" button to start creating the accounting file

Note

You can change the information entered when creating the accounting file in the file properties in the File menu, Open, click on Properties. The properties of the selected file will be displayed.

CHAPTER VII

STORAGE MEMORY CONCEPT

VII.1.DEFINITION

A "**memory**" is any electronic component capable of temporarily storing data.

VII.2.ROLE

1. **mass memory,** whose role is to be a permanent storage area. This role is performed by the disks
(hard disks, SSDs, floppy disks, CD-ROMs or DVDs) or magnetic tapes. Data is recorded using magnetic, electronic or optical processes, and remains even when the equipment is switched off. However, these systems are relatively slow.

2. **the central memory**, whose role is to act as a work area
and temporary storage. The programs you want to run and the data you want to process must first be loaded into main memory so that they are available to the processor.

VII .3.TYPES OF MEMORY

A. LIVING MEMORY

Random *Access* **Memory** (**RAM)** is the system's main memory, i.e. the space used to temporarily store data while a program is running.

Unlike storing data on a mass memory device such as a hard disk, RAM is volatile, meaning that it can only store data for as long as it is powered. So, each time the computer is switched off, all the data in the memory is irremediably erased.

B. DEAD MEMORY

Read-only **memory** *(***ROM)** is a type of memory that retains the information it contains even when the memory is no longer powered. Basically, this type of memory can only be accessed in read mode. However, it is now possible to record information in certain *ROM-type* memories.

C. FLASH MEMORY

Flash memory is a compromise between RAM and read-only memory. Flash memory has the non-volatility of read-only memories, while still being easily accessible for reading or writing. On the other hand, flash memory access times are longer than those of RAM.

CHAPTER VIII

TABLE NOTION (in Microsoft Word)

VIII.1 INSERTION

For a basic table, click on **Insert> Table** and move the cursor over the grid to highlight the desired number of columns and rows.

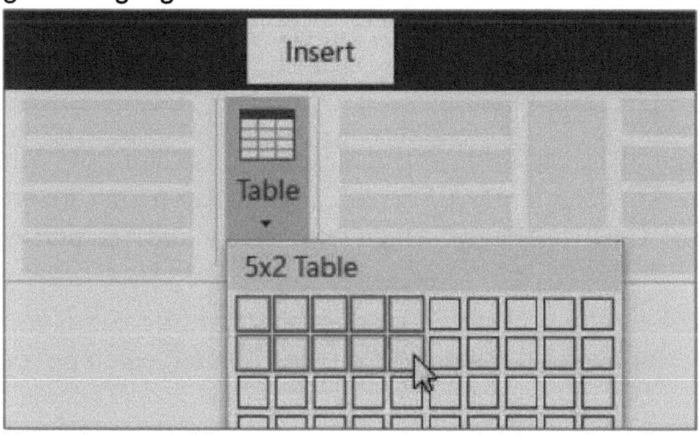

For a larger table or to customise a table, select **Insert> Table> Insert a table**.

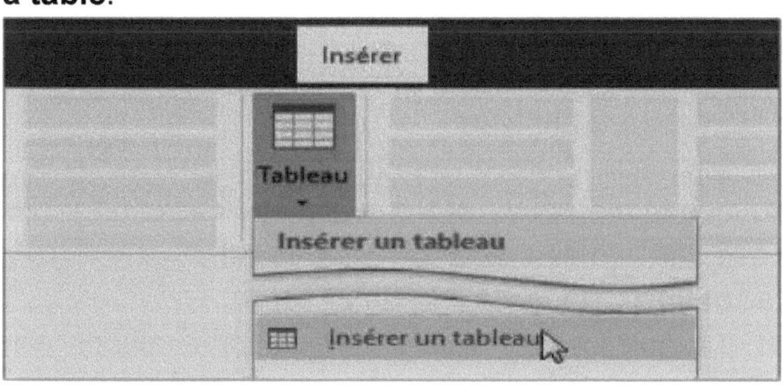

Advice :

- If you already have text separated by tabs, you can quickly convert it into a table. Select **Insert> Table**, then select **Convert text to table**.
- To draw your own table, select **Insert> table> draw a table**.

VIII.2.MODIFICATION

A table in Microsoft Word can organise numerical or textual information. Microsoft Word 2007 includes the "Table Tools" menu, which appears on the Ribbon at the top of the screen when you activate a table. You can use the "Layout" tab of the function to modify the table by adding or deleting cells, rows and columns. Instructions

1. Click on the table. The "Table Tools" menu appears at the far right of

the Ribbon. Click on the "Layout" tab.

2. Add a cell to a single horizontal row by clicking on the cell to the right of where you want the new cell. Press the small arrow in the bottom right-hand corner of the "Rows and columns" menu. Click on "Shift right" and press "OK".

3. Delete a cell on a single horizontal row by clicking on its left-hand side to select it. Press the "Delete" button and select "Delete cells". "Click on "Shift right" and press "OK".

4. Add a row or column by clicking on a cell adjacent to the one you want to add the row or column to. Click on "Insert above" or "Insert below" to add a row. Click on "Insert Right" or "Insert Left" to add a column.

5. delete a row or column by clicking on a cell in the row or column you wish to delete. Press the "Delete" button and choose "Delete columns" or "Delete rows. "

6. Modify in the table by placing the cursor to the right of the data you want to change in an individual cell. Press the "Delete" key to delete the old data, then type in the new data.

VIII.3.FORMATTING

Step 1: Access the "Create a table" tab

Once you are in your Microsoft Word document, click on the table you want to format. If you look in the ribbon at the top of the Microsoft Word application, you can see that two new tabs have appeared.

We are only interested in the "**Create a table**" tab.

The '**Create a panel**' tab gives you the colour and border options you need to modify the appearance of your selected panel. Click on it to get started.

The menu in the '**Table creation**' tab is divided into three parts: '**Table style options**', '**Table styles**' and '**Borders**'.

Step 2: Modify the table style options

"**Table Style Options**" allows you to modify the result of the styles in "**Table Styles**". "**Header row**" allows you to start the first row of your table, "**Total row**" starts the last row of your table, "**First column**" starts the leftmost row of your table, "**Last column**" starts the rightmost row of your table, "**Striped rows**" puts a darker background on every other row and finally "**Striped columns**" puts a darker background on every other column.

For our table, we have chosen to tick only "**Header line**" and "**Striped**

lines".

Step 3: Apply a style to your table

Now that we've chosen our options, we can choose a style.

Microsoft Word offers a number of pre-made table styles. To see them all easily, click on the button with the line and arrow pointing down.

You can get an idea of what a style would look like on your painting just by hovering your mouse over the style you're interested in.

Once you have chosen your style, click on it to apply it to your table.

If you want to change the background of a particular cell, select it and then click on **"Background"**. Microsoft Word will ask you to choose the colour you want to apply to the background of the cells you have selected.

Step 4: Modify the borders of your table

If you want to add or change the borders of your table, go to "**Borders**". Click on "**Border layout**" and then click on the cells whose borders you want to change. Press the **Esc** key or click on "**Borders layout**" again.

To change the appearance of the borders you apply, you can click on '**Border styles**' to see the different basic border styles in Microsoft Word, or click on the fields to the right of '**Border styles**' to customise the appearance, thickness and colour of the borders you place.

Also, if you use '**Border**', you can choose which border of the cells you modify with '**Border formatting**'. Basically, "**Border**" will be set to modify the bottom border of the cell.

VIII.4.PRINTING

To print a document, click on the **File** tab and **the screen** appears.

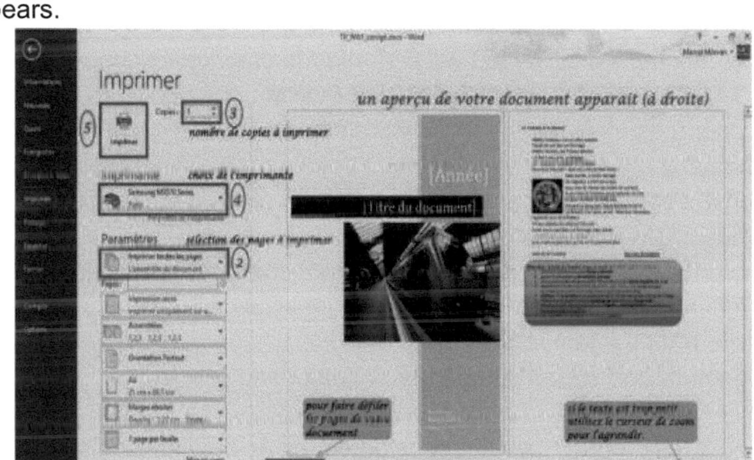

Perform the following actions:

1. click on **Print** in the blue banner on the left
2. select the pages to be printed: by default, **all pages are printed**, but you can make your own selection by clicking on the **right arrow** to see the other options.
3. select the **number of copies** of your document you wish to print
4. select the **printer** to be used for printing
5. start printing by pressing the **Print** button.

Click on (in the blue banner on the left) to return to your document.

VIII.5.APPLICATIONS LEADING TO THE PREPARATION OF THE PURCHASE ORDER AND INVOICE

The purchase order is a commercial document drawn up by the seller. It sets out the details of the order and serves to formalise the intention to buy. Producing a purchase order is by no means compulsory and has no accounting value. In fact, a sale can be concluded verbally as soon as the seller and buyer have reached agreement on the price, products and quantities.

To create purchase orders, you can download templates online. However, it is also possible to draw up purchase orders in Word or Excel. However, when there are a lot of purchase orders to be drawn up, it can take a long time to type them in.

That's why it's a good idea to use commercial management software (such as HubSpot, EBP, Sage, Sellsy or Oxygene) with a range of possible forms (quotes, invoices, etc.). Some of this software is free, while others have to be paid for.

The company will save a great deal of time thanks to the simplicity of the various functions offered, but will first need to draw up its customer files.

CHARACTERISTICS OF THE ORDER FORM

The order form includes the following elements:

- company name, name and contact details of the issuer (customer) ;
- contact details, company name and name of recipient (supplier) ;
- a description of the products or services ordered;
- the price of the products or services (not compulsory but recommended);
- preferred payment terms ;
- signature and stamp of the person authorised to sign to order.

The purchase order can be considered as a binding contract if it is

signed by the issuer and countersigned by the supplier.
But in most cases, orders are placed without any formality, and therefore without a purchase order. A simple e-mail can be sent to the supplier, who then takes charge of formalising the order and having it validated by the customer in the form of a quotation or a pro forma invoice, or even a final invoice.

EXAMPLE OF AN ORDER FORM

ORDER FORM

Company name (corporate form and name)
A :
No client Address
Amount of share capital
RCS number and location
Head office address Telephone
Purchase order number :
Date :

REF	DESCRIPTI ON	QUT E	P.U HT	REMI SE	TOT AL HT	Taux de TVA	TOTAL TTC
Article 1		1	250,00 $		250, 00 $	20,0%	300,00 $
Article 2		5	100,00 $	20%	400, 00 $	5,5%	422,00 $
					- $		- $
					- $		- $
				TOTA	650, 00 $		722,00 $

Terms of delivery:
Terms of payment :
Withdrawal period :

CHAPTER IX

REMINDER

IX.1.STARTING THE COMPUTER (practical)

IX.2.LAUNCHING MS WORD (practice at the computer)

IX.3.PRESENTATION OF THE WORD INTERFACE (title bar, scroll bar, formatting tools) :

IX.3.1.DATA ENTRY (TYPING BY THE KILOMETRE)

Typing by the kilometre (also called "typing by the kilometre") is a working method which consists of **writing your text without worrying about formatting** (at least not too much). Understand that when writing a document in Word, you type your text concentrating mainly on the content, on the message you want to get across to your reader. This applies equally to a covering letter, a memoir, an administrative document , a complaint, a job application, a collection of recipes, a book... and any other type of document.

IX.3.2.CORRECTING TEXT WHILE TYPING

Word has a high-performance spelling and grammar checker. It **detects and highlights the** most common spelling and grammar **errors**. This automatic Word checker can be used to correct a long document before sending it to the recipient.

To **correct a spelling mistake**, right-click on the underlined word and choose one of the replacement words suggested by Word. The misspelled word is automatically corrected in Word. Misspelled words are underlined with a red wavy line, indicating that they are not present in Word's dictionary.

If you want to **add to your dictionary** and have Word automatically correct it with a complete French dictionary, simply add them manually. To do this, right-click on the word and select "Add to dictionary" from the context menu. Your vocabulary will then be added to the spelling correction in your Word software.

IX.3.3.RECORDING A TEXT

To save a document in Word, there are two tabs: Either in the small icon at the very top of the software,

Either in "file" then click on "save" or "save as" :

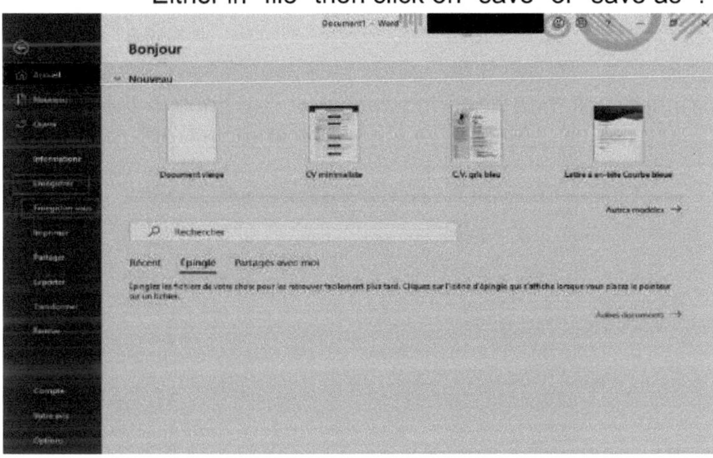

Either by clicking on the "control" key and "S" if you are on a computer, or the "command" key and "S" if you are on a Mac.

CHANGE DOCUMENT NAME, LOCATION AND FORMAT

To change the name, location or format of your Word document, click on "Browse". A window will then open allowing you to choose the location where you want to save your document, as well as the document title and format. The most commonly used formats for saving documents are "doc.x", "pdf", "RTF", "TXT", or ".html". However, the format can be changed from one computer to another. The PDF format retains the formatting on each computer.

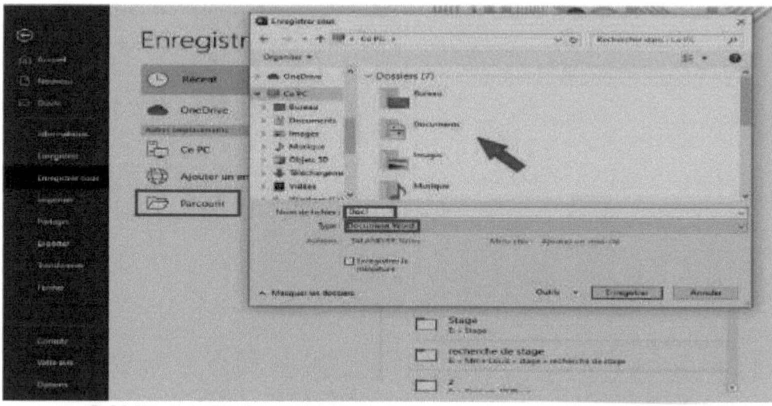

SAVE A NEW VERSION OF A WORD DOCUMENT

To save a new version of a Word document, simply use the "save as" function. To do this, go to "File" and click on "Save as", then on "Browse". A window will then open in which you can choose the location where you want to save your document, as well as the document title and format.

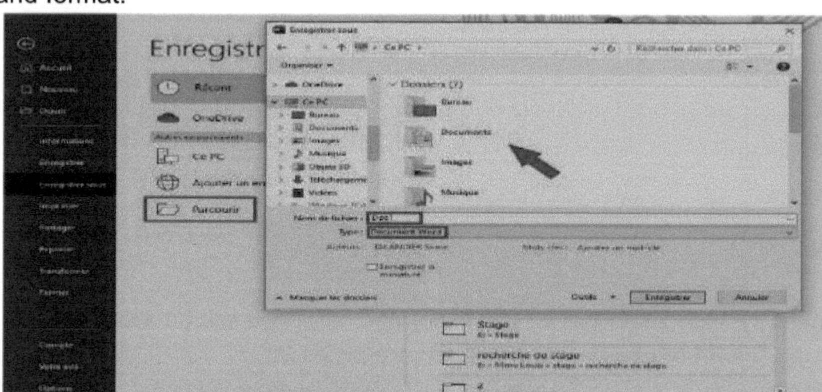

IX.3.4.OPENING A DOCUMENT

There are 2 main ways of opening an existing document:

- You can either find it in your folders and double-click on the icon to open it. Don't worry if the programme isn't open, everything will be done automatically.

- Either the program is already open, in which case you use the "**Open**" command in the "**File**" tab:

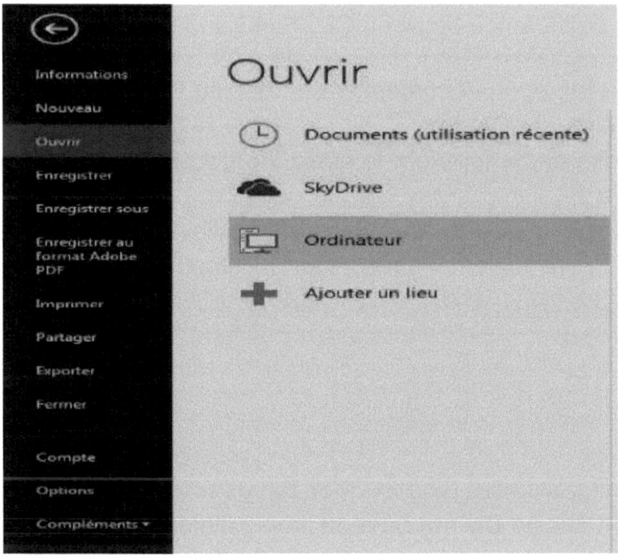

By clicking on "**Computer**", you can browse your tree to find your file and open it by clicking on "**Open**".
If it's a document you've used recently, you'll find it in the "**Documents (recent use)"** list, which makes it much easier to find!

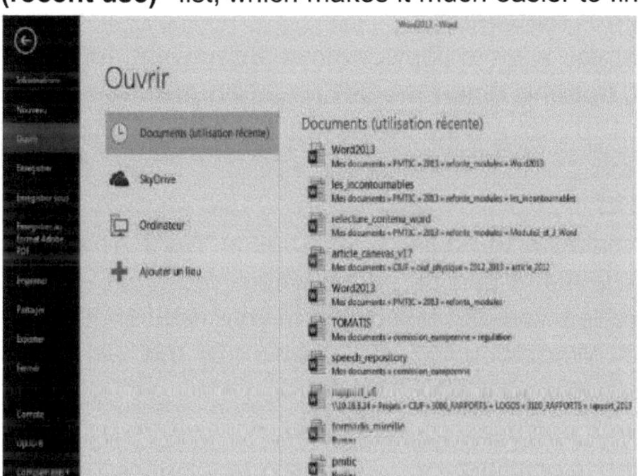

IX.3.5.CLOSING A DOCUMENT

To quit Word, simply close the cross at the top right or go to the bar above the banner, click on the Word Icon and then on "**Close**":

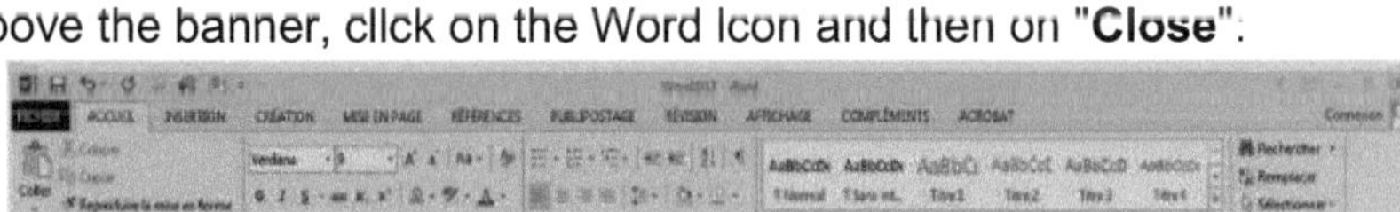

Please note! There's a difference between CLOSING and LEAVING:

Close: you can close the open document while keeping Word open. Go to the "**File**" tab and click on "**Close**".
Quit: click on the cross at the top right to close the document you have open AND Word.
Warning: if you get the message "Do you want to save the changes made to Document1?", you have not saved your document.

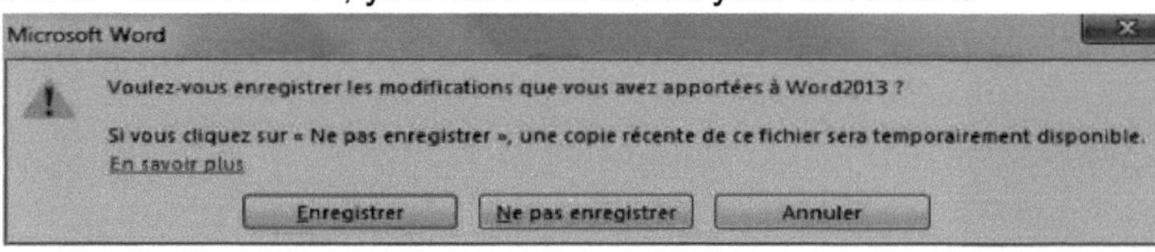

Click **Save** to save the document (you will then have to name it, see "the page about saving"). Click on **Do not save** to save nothing (you will lose everything you have done in this document). Click **Cancel** if you have clicked on the cross by mistake and want to keep your document open.

IX.3.6.PRINTING A TEXT

(cfr notion on table, chapter VIII)

IX.3.7.MOVING WITHIN A DOCUMENT

In Word, select the text you want to copy or move. To move it, **left-click on the selection and, holding down the left mouse button, drag it to the position you want to move it to**. Release the mouse button. Your text is moved.

IX.3.8.INSERTING TEXT

There are several advantages to adding a text box in Word. The great thing about a text box is that it can be added where you don't want to highlight text. MS Office lets you add text boxes to your documents. This means that, apart from Word, you can also add a text box with other Office applications. The process is explained below.

1. First, access the Word document to get started.
2. Press the "Insert" tab to continue.
3. You now need to press the "Text box" option under the tab to create a text box on the document. You will be presented with several options. It is advisable to choose the one that best suits your needs. This depends entirely on the type of document you are creating or the needs of the presentation you are making. Just bear in mind that your text box needs to look professional.

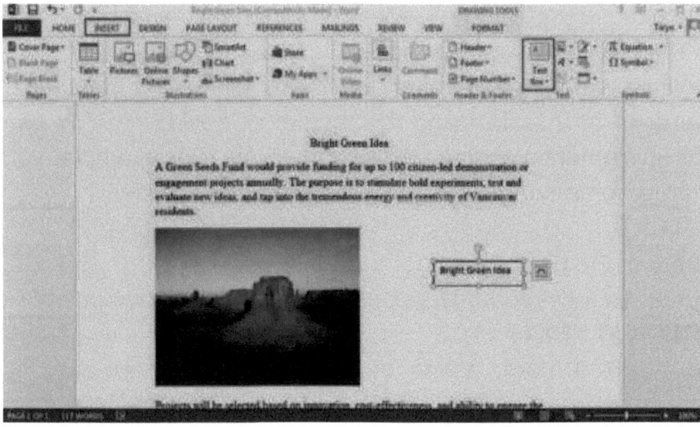

1. Click on the option you want to add to the document. Next, go to the "Format" tab and click on "Shape border", then on "No border" if you don't want to define a border.

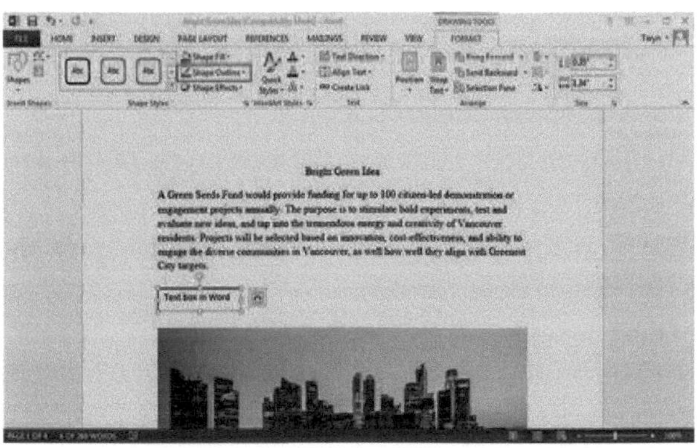

You can now click on the text box to access the drawing toolbar at the top. If you need to make any changes, everything is on the toolbar.

- You can insert different shapes into the text box and you can also draw a new text box.
- You can also apply different shape styles to the text area that has been added to the Word document
- Add Word Art styles and make sure you get the best alignment.
- You can also arrange the text box as you wish.
- To delete the text box, simply click on the edge of the text box, then click Delete. The box will be permanently deleted.

Note: It is very important to note that from Word 2007 onwards, the method for applying the text box is the same. Older versions of Word are not mentioned because they are no longer supported by Microsoft .®

IX.3.9.SELECTING A TEXT

In Word, you can select all the text in a document (Ctrl+A), or select text or specific elements of a table using the mouse or keyboard. You can also select text or elements located at different points. For example, you can select a paragraph on one page and a sentence on another.

SELECT ALL TEXT

1. Click anywhere in the document.
2. Press Ctrl+A on your keyboard to select all the text in the document.

SELECT A SPECIFIC TEXT

You can also select a word, a line of text or one or more specific paragraphs.

1. Place your cursor in front of the first letter of the word, sentence or paragraphs you want to select.
2. Click and hold the mouse button while you drag the cursor to select the text of your choice.

OTHER WAYS OF SELECTING TEXT

- To select a single word, quickly double-click on it.
- To select a line of text, place your cursor at the beginning of the line, then press Shift+Arrow down.
- To select a paragraph, place your cursor at the beginning of the paragraph, then press Ctrl+Shift+Down arrow.

IX.3.10.DELETING A TEXT

To delete text, simply click on the border of the text box you wish to delete and press Delete.

Note: Make sure that the pointer is on the edge of the text box and not inside it. If the pointer is inside the box, pressing Delete deletes the text inside the text box, not the box.

IX.3.11.COPYING A TEXT (COPY/PASTE)

Copy/paste is the action of duplicating a file from one location to another. The file is then cloned from its origin to a new destination. Copy and paste is performed, for example, by right-clicking on a selection and choosing "Copy", then right-clicking and "Paste" in the destination folder. The keyboard shortcuts for this action are Ctrl+C and Ctrl+V. Copy and paste is used, for example, to copy the contents of a folder to a USB key.

IX.3.12.CORRECTING A REPEATED WORD IN THE ENTERED TEXT SET

One of the most common mistakes made when writing a document is that words are sometimes repeated. Normally, Word's automatic checker warns you of this error by underlining the repetition in red. But this is not infallible, and if you have deactivated the correction tool, it is still possible to detect these errors very easily. Using the program's wildcards.

IX.3.13.SPELL CHECKING

To check spelling in MS Word, simply :

Click or tap on the location where you want to add text, or select the text you want to mark as being in another language, then do one of the following:

1. Under the **Revision** tab, select **Language>** **Preferences linguistics**.
2. Under the **Languages of creation and verification** **linguistics d'Office**, select the language you want to use.
3. Select **OK**.

Or

1. In the **Revision** tab, select **Language>** **Define the verification language**.
2. Select the desired language.
3. Select **OK**.

Tip: To avoid having to manually set the proofreading language with each new document in Word, switch to the option that detects the language you are writing in. In the **Revision** tab, go to **Language**. Choose **Language>** **Define the language for linguistic verification**,

IX.3.14.REPLACING A WORD WITH ANOTHER WORD

If you want to replace one word with another throughout your Word document, click on the **Edit** menu and then on the **Replace** command (Ctrl+ H).

In the **Search** field, type the word to search for, then in the **Replace with** field, enter the replacement word.

Finally, click on the **Replace** All button to perform the operation throughout your document.

IX.3.15.REPLACEMENT OF A WORD BY ANOTHER SYNONYMOUS WORD

Simply select the word to be replaced, then right-click, then go to **Synonyms.** Word will suggest a list of synonyms for the word. Simply select one from the list to use it.

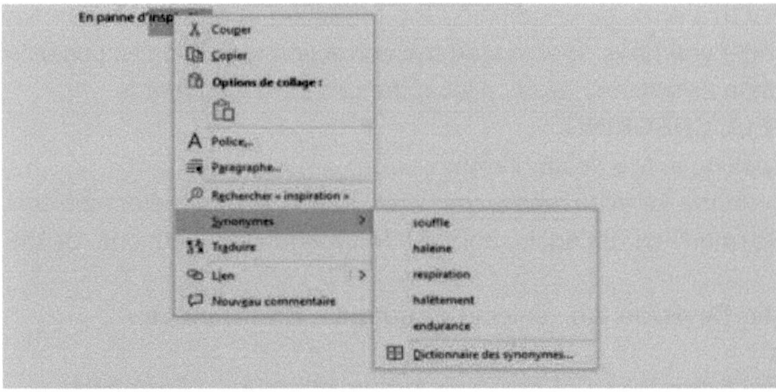
Couper
Copier
Options de collage :
Police...
Paragraphe...
Rechercher « inspiration »
Synonymes
Traduire
Lien
Nouveau commentaire
souffle
haleine
respiration
halètement
endurance
Dictionnaire des synonymes...

CHAPTER X

GENERAL INFORMATION ABOUT THE INTERNET

X.1.BACKGROUND

The first texts describing the social interactions that could be made possible by a computer network were a series of memos written by J.C.R. Licklider of MIT in August 1962 on his concept of the "galactic network". He imagined a set of globally interconnected computers through which anyone could quickly access data and programmes from any location. In theory, the concept was very similar to today's Internet. Licklider was the first head of DARPA's computer research programme, launched in October 1962. During his time at DARPA, he persuaded his successors, Ivan Sutherland, Bob Taylor and Lawrence G.

Roberts, a researcher at MIT, of the interest of this computer network concept.

Leonard Kleinrock of MIT published the first paper on the use of packet switching in July 1961 and the first book on the subject in 1964. Kleinrock convinced Roberts of the theoretical realisation of communications using packet switching rather than dedicated circuits, which proved to be a major step towards computer networks. Another key step was to enable computers to communicate with each other.

In 1965, in order to explore this, with the help of Thomas Merrill, Roberts connected the TX-2 computer in Massachusetts with the Q-32 computer in California via a low-speed switched telephone link, creating the first (albeit very small) network extended computer ever built. This experiment proved that time-sharing computers could work together very well, running programs and retrieving data if necessary from the remote machine, but that the switched telephone system was totally inadequate. Kleinrock's belief in the need for packet switching was confirmed.

At the end of 1966, Roberts was hired by DARPA to develop the computer network concept and quickly put in place his plan for the "ARPANET" network, which he published in 1967. At the conference where he presented the paper, a presentation on a packet switched network concept was also given by Donald Davies and Roger Scantlebury of the UK's NPL. Scantlebury told Roberts about NPL's work and that of Paul Baran and others at RAND. The RAND group had written a paper on the use of a packet-switched network for secure transmission voice in the military in 1964. As it happened, the work carried out at MIT (1961-1967), RAND (1962-1965) and NPL (1964-1967) all took place in parallel, without any of the researchers being aware of the others' work. The word "packet" was adopted from the work at NPL and the proposed transmission speed to be used in the design of ARPANET was improved from 2.4 kbps to 50 kbps.

In August 1968, having refined the general structure and specifications of the ARPANET network, Roberts and DARPA issued a call for tenders for the production of a key component of the network: packet switches called Interface Message Processors (IMPs). Bolt Beranek and Newman (BBN), headed by Frank Heart, won the tender in December 1968. While the BBN team worked on the IMPs with Bob Kahn, playing a key role in the architectural design of the ARPANET network, the network topology and economics were designed and optimised by Roberts working with Howard Frank and his team at Network Analysis Corporation, and the network measurement system was prepared by Professor Kleinrock's team at UCLA.

Thanks to Kleinrock's early development of packet switching theory and his focus on analysis, design and measurement, his Network Measurement Center at UCLA was chosen to be the first node on the ARPANET. In September 1969, BBN installed the first IMP network equipment at UCLA and the first host computer was connected. Doug Engelbart's Augmenting Human Intelligence project (which included the first hypertext system, NLS) at the Stanford Research Institute (SRI) provided a second node. The SRI supported the Network Information Center, headed by Elizabeth (Jake) Feinler and including functions such as maintaining tables of hostnames and addresses and a directory of RFCs.

A month later, when SRI was connected to the ARPANET network, the first host-to-host message was sent from Kleinrock's laboratory to SRI. Two more nodes were added at the University of Santa Barbara (UCSB) and the University of Utah. These last two nodes incorporated application visualisation projects, with Glen Culler and Burton Fried at UCSB studying methods of displaying mathematical functions using memory screens to cope with the problem of refreshment on the network, and Robert Taylor and Ivan Sutherland at the University of Utah studying methods of 3D representations on the network. So, by the end of 1969, the initial ARPANET network consisted of four host computers and the Internet was born. Even at this early stage, it should be noted that network research integrated both work on the underlying network and work on how to use the network. This tradition continues to this day.

Computers were quickly added to the ARPANET network over the next few years, and work continued on completing a functionally complete host-to-host communications protocol and other network software. In December 1970, the Network Working Group (NWG), led by S. Crocker, completed the host-to-host communications protocol for the ARPANET network, called the Network Control Protocol or NCP. As ARPANET sites finished implementing NCP between 1971 and 1972, network users were finally able to develop the first applications.

In October 1972, Kahn organised a major and highly successful demonstration of the ARPANET network at the International Conference on Computer Communications (ICCC). This was the first public demonstration of the new technology. It was also in 1972 that the first major application was developed: electronic mail. In March, Ray Tomlinson at BBN wrote the first basic software for sending and receiving e-mail, thus meeting the communication needs of ARPANET network developers. In July, Roberts extended his application by writing the first e-mail program to list, selectively read, classify, route and reply to messages. From there, e-mail took off as the largest network application for over a decade. It was a harbinger of the kind of activity we see on the World Wide Web today, namely the huge growth in traffic of all kinds connecting people.

X.2.DEFINITION

Main Internet services (www, mail, FTP, chat, telephones) Main browsers (Internet Explorer, Mozilla, Opera, etc.)

Internet access (via the desktop, the status bar or the program menu)

Search engine(Google)

X.3.MAIN INTERNET SERVICES

X.3.1.WWW

The WWW, or World Wide Web, is a global information system available at . It allows users to consult documents, navigate from one page to another, and access various types of multimedia content via hypertext links. In other words, it is a network of interconnected web pages accessible via the Internet.

THE HISTORY OF THE WORLD WIDE WEB

The WWW was invented by Sir Tim Berners-Lee in 1989. Its original purpose was to facilitate the sharing of information between scientists and researchers around the world. The first website was created in 1991, marking the beginning of the **WWW** era.

HOW WWW WORKS

The WWW operates using a protocol called HTTP (Hypertext Transfer

Protocol). When you enter a web address into your browser, it sends a request to the corresponding web server via HTTP. The server then sends the requested web page back to your browser, which displays it on your screen. This process takes place in a fraction of a second.

WWW COMPONENTS

The WWW is made up of several essential components, including web browsers, web servers, web pages, hypertext links and communication protocols. These components work together to provide a seamless browsing experience.

THE IMPORTANCE OF THE WWW IN EVERYDAY LIFE

The WWW has revolutionised the way we live and work. It allows us to access an infinite amount of information, shop online, watch videos, communicate with friends and colleagues, and much more. It has also opened up new opportunities for businesses and entrepreneurs.

THE ADVANTAGES AND DISADVANTAGES OF WWW

Although the WWW has brought many benefits, it has also had its drawbacks. Advantages include access to information, global communication and business opportunities. However, the disadvantages include online security problems, misinformation and over-reliance on the Internet.

X.3.2.MAIL

E-mail refers to electronic mail, i.e. a message written and sent electronically via a computer network. The e-mail is sent from one electronic mailbox to another.

X.3.3.FTP

In the IT world, we often hear the term FTP. The acronym FTP stands for File Transfer Protocol, a protocol used to transfer files from a computer to a server or from a server to a computer... But not just any files! Those that are too large to be sent from another location (the files on your website, for example).

X.3.4.CHAT

Instant messaging (*chat*) enables people connected to the network to talk directly to each other by exchanging texts, which are generally very short and often written in a jargon based on abbreviations and graphic symbols.

X.3.5.TELEPHONE

The telephone is a communications device originally designed to transmit the human voice and communicate at a distance. To operate, the telephone requires a terrestrial or space infrastructure: the telephone network.

X.4.MAIN BROWSERS

Web browsers are software programs that allow you to consult web pages and Internet sites. They are the gateway to the Internet and all the pages available.

The best web browsers are Google Chrome, Mozilla Firefox, Microsoft Edge (formerly Internet Explorer), Safari, Brave, Opera, Tor Browser, Vivaldi and Sidekick. The user interface is generally customisable, so you can simplify browsing with intuitive interfaces. Web browsers can be used on the desktop (Windows, macOS or Linux) as well as on mobile devices (iOS, Android), thanks to the mobile versions.

The main functions offered by web browsers are as follows:

- **Multiple tabs:** you can have a large number of tabs open at the same time to switch from one website to another without losing progress.
- **Password management:** the web browser can store your password (only with your agreement) in a secure manner, so that it can be pre-filled the next time you visit the site.
- **Security:** most web browsers offer regular, automatic updates to combat malicious attacks and prevent security breaches. They also offer other functions, such as pop-up blocking or warnings if you visit a potentially dangerous site or download something suspicious.
- **Confidentiality of personal data:** to ensure the protection of your your personal data, the browsers allow management of advertising tracking to control cookies and the use of private browsing.
- **Add shortcuts/favourites:** you can add several sites to a list of favourites or bookmarks, to access them more quickly, without having to use a search engine.
- **Integration of web extensions :** browsers offer generally the ability to add custom extensions or plugins, such as ad blockers, productivity tools (screen capture, file converter, translator, etc.) and development tools, or even extensions dedicated to videoconferencing tools.
- **Downloads:** elements that can be downloaded from websites are saved in the browser.
- **PDF integration:** you can read, edit and share PDFs directly from web browsers.
- **VPN:** some browsers, such as Opera or Sidekick, include a VPN to protect your personal information when you surf the web.

- **Browsing data:** browsers allow you to consult browsing history and manage or delete browsing data.
- **Address bar:** you can access websites directly from the browser's search bar, which lets you type in the exact address of a site, or keywords that will launch a search on your default search engine.

CHOOSE A WEB BROWSER

Browsers are regularly updated to be faster and to support the latest versions of websites. To choose your browser, you need to determine your needs in terms of privacy protection, plugins, speed and compatibility. Some older browsers may not be compatible with certain new versions of websites. Sometimes technologies change, and browsers and sites have to adapt, as was the case with the end of Adobe Flash Player. Mobile browsers are available to download from the various stores, or are sometimes preinstalled, like Apple's Safari for example.

THE BEST NAVIGATOR RANKING IN NOVEMBER 2023 :

1. Opera
2. Mozilla Firefox
3. Google Chrome
4. Microsoft Edge
5. Vivaldi

X.5.INTERNET ACCESS

X.5.1.BY THE BUREAU

1. Select **the** network or **Wifi icon** in the notification area.
2. In the list of networks, choose the network you want to connect to, then select **Connect**.
3. Enter the security key (often called the password).
4. Follow any additional instructions.

If you have problems with your Wi-Fi network when using Windows 10, see Solving Wi-Fi problems in Windows_for advanced troubleshooting information.

X.5.2.VIA THE STATUS BAR

1. Select the **Network** icon in the taskbar. The icon displayed depends on your current connection status. If you don't see any of the network icons (or a similar icon) displayed in the following image, select the **up arrow** to see if it appears.

2. Choose the Wi-Fi network you want to connect to, then select **Connect**.
3. Enter the network password, then select **Next**.
4. Choose **Yes** or **No**, depending on the type of network you are connecting to and whether you want your PC to be detectable by other PCs and devices on the network.

X.6.SEARCH ENGINE (Google)

X.7.E-MAIL

Electronic mail, **e-mail** or **email/e-mail**, is a service for transmitting messages sent electronically via a computer network (mainly the Internet) to the electronic mailbox of a recipient chosen by the sender .[7]

X.7.1.CREATION

HOW TO CREATE A GMAIL ACCOUNT

The first step in creating a Gmail account is to go to the Gmail page on your search engine. Then click on the "***Create an account***" tab and enter your first and last name. Once you've completed these first few fields, **enter your username and password**. For security reasons, always choose a password that is sufficiently complex and different from your other accounts. You will then be asked to **confirm your password again** by entering it a second time. You can also enter your date of birth and telephone number, although these are not compulsory. Finally, all you have to do is accept the terms of use of the service to validate your account and access the user interface.

THE COMPOSITION OF AN E-MAIL ADDRESS

An email address is made up of a set of components that can be used to communicate and send all possible media (document, video, image, file, etc.).

[7] https://www.techno-science.net, consulted on 14/11/2023 at 03h27'

The components of an e-mail address are the identifier, which is generally the surname, first name and special characters such as hyphens, dots and the arobase separator **(@)**. Then, to conclude the email address, you either choose to add your domain name or the name of your company or simply leave the name of the email address provider (Gmail, Yahoo, Bing, etc.). Finally, when it comes to passwords, we recommend a mix of letters, special characters and numbers. And make a note of this password somewhere on your phone.

X.7.2.SEND

Sending an e-mail is fairly straightforward. First of all, you need to log in to your e-mail account and click on the "new message" button. Next, you need to enter the email address of the person you want to send the message to, the subject of the message and the body of the message. You can also add attachments such as files, images or videos. Finally, click on the "send" button to send the message.

X.7.3.DISCONNECTION

LOGGING OFF A COMPUTER

1. Open Gmail.
2. In the top right-hand corner, click on your photo.
3. Click on **Logout**.

DISCONNECTING ON ANOTHER DEVICE

If you've forgotten to log out of your mailbox on another computer, you can log out of Gmail remotely.

1. Open Gmail.
2. In the top right-hand corner, click on your photo.
3. Click on **Manage your Google Account**.
4. Click on **Security**.
5. Under "Your devices", click on **Manage all devices**.
6. Select a device.
7. Click on **Logout**.

X.7.4.ACCESS

This solution is very simple and works just as well on a computer (Windows, Mac, Linux) as it does on a smartphone or tablet (without the need to install an application). The downside is that you may need to log in regularly (giving your email address and password).

Gmail login box **on a web browser**

To access your Gmail account in a web browser :

1. open the page www.gmail.com
2. if prompted, type the email address of your Gmail account, ending with @gmail.com, then click Next
3. enter your Gmail password and click Next
4. you arrive in your Gmail inbox

Remarks :

- if you were already connected to Gmail in your browser, you don't need to identify yourself by entering your email address and password. In this case, check that it's the right account. If not, you'll need to sign out of Gmail .first
- The exact address of Google's email service is https://mail.google.com/mail/u/0/#inbox but you can access it by simply typing gmail.com or gmail.fr (with or without www it's all the same), or mail.google.com.

X.7.5.ANSWER

To reply to e-mail messages, simply follow the steps below:

1. Open the Gmail >*< application on your Android phone or tablet.
2. Open the message.
3. At the bottom of the message, press :

- **Reply**: send the message to the sender.
- **Reply to all**: send the message to the sender and to all the people on

the "A" and "Cc" lines.

4. Enter your message.
5. Press Send .>

X.7.1.6.PRINTING

1. Select the message to print.
2. At the top of the page, select > **Print**.

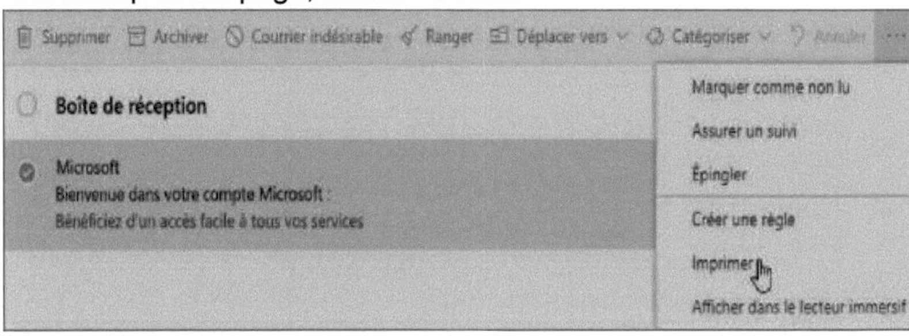

3. A preview of your message opens in a new window. At the top of the window, select **Print**.
4. In the **Print dialog box**, choose the options then select **Print**.

PRINT ATTACHMENTS

To print attachments, you can download and save them on your local computer or on OneDrive and open them with the appropriate program. For example, you can open and print .doc files from Word and open and print .pdf files from Adobe Reader.

1. Open the message containing the attachment you wish to print.
2. Under the attachment, select **Download**.

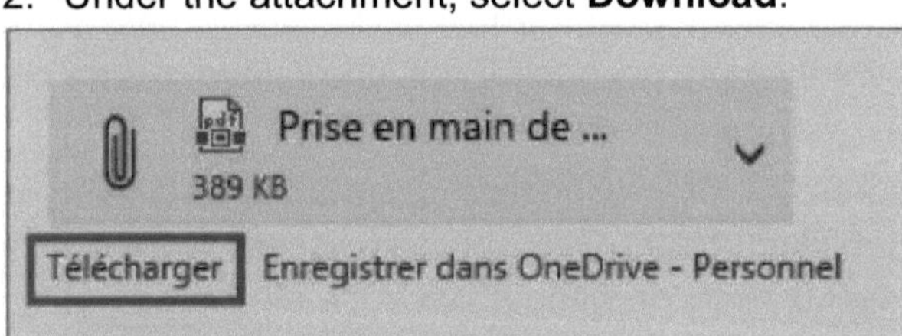

3. After downloading the file, open it in the appropriate program and select the print option. For example, open a .doc file in Word, then print it.

BIBLIOGRAPHY

❖ **The books :**

- Curriculum National des Humanites Techniques Commercials, March 2014;
- Jacques LONCHAMP, introduction aux systemes informatique, Paris, Dunod, 2011.

❖ **Websites :**

- https://www.futura-sciences.com
- https://www.synonyme-du-mot.com
- https://www.maxicours.com
- https://www.techno-science.net
- https://barrazacarlos.com
- https://www.larousse.fr

MIX
Papier aus verantwortungsvollen Quellen
Paper from responsible sources
FSC® C105338

Printed by Books on Demand GmbH, Norderstedt / Germany